# you can two!

# YOU CAN two!

## The Essential Twins Preparation Guide

Jennifer Bonicelli & Meghan Hertzfeldt

ILLUSTRATIONS BY EMMELINE PIDGEN

ROCKRIDGE PRESS

To our miracle babies, our *two came true,* our beautiful gifts of unrelenting love.

Interior and Cover Designer: Katy Brown
Editor: Stacy Wagner-Kinnear
Production Editor: Erum Khan
Illustrations © Emmeline Pidgen, 2018
Author photos © Jenna Sparks Photography

ISBN: Print 978-1-64152-178-9 | eBook 978-1-64152-179-6

# Contents

# Introduction

**WELCOME, TWIN PARENTS-TO-BE!** We wish we could jump out of these pages to give you a huge congratulatory hug. That's how excited we are for each and every one of you. Oh, and since we're practically hugging, we might as well introduce ourselves. We're Jenn and Meghan, co-founders of the blog *Two Came True*, which we developed to be an online community and resource center for twin parents. We provide content and guidance to help twin parents feel confident and enjoy the wild ride that is parenting multiples. We're also twin moms ourselves, so we've been where you are and have learned a thing or two about this twin parenting gig.

You might think that our shared struggles with infertility (yup) or that our boys (yup, we each have a set of fraternal twin sons) brought us together, but that's not the case. We met as teachers in 2009, before either of us had children. Teachers are planners by nature. And trust us, no matter how much we'd plan, something would inevitably happen to change those plans, and we'd just have to adapt. All. The. Time. But the good news is that by making a plan, you know the goal you want to accomplish. When the chaos does ensue, you can be flexible and make adjustments as long as you keep that goal in mind. Parenting twins, it turns out, isn't so different.

Few of us feel prepared to be parents of twins when we first receive the news. Along the way, there are incredible highs and often some pretty epic fails. There isn't a recipe for perfect parenting, but we all can benefit from a little preparation. This book is filled with practical information and advice to educate and empower you as you get ready for your adventure with twins. We've taken our experiences as educators, twin parents, and parenting consultants to give you a Mary Poppins–size bag of parenting tricks.

*You Can Two!* is designed to be an action-oriented guide to read during pregnancy (or soon after delivery) that covers how to tackle everything that happens in the first few months after your babies arrive. You'll find ways to preemptively strengthen your relationship, care for your finances, gather the gear that you need (and know what you don't need), help you keep two tiny humans fed, teach them to sleep, and keep the parent team intact while you navigate twinfancy. Whoa, that's a lot! We know, but take a deep breath—we cover it all, step by step. We've also included a schedule tracker, two big charts, and lots of checklists in this book, which you can use throughout the first several months. Feel free to write directly in the book or download them at CallistoMediaBooks.com/YouCanTwo.

While there is no one-size-fits-all approach to parenting, it certainly helps to have strategies and recommendations from those who've been there. Beyond the guidance we provide, we've included anecdotes and tips from experts and other parents of twins, reminding us that raising twins is a unique and wonderful gift. We hope that their words will excite you in the months before your twins arrive, and that the practical strategies they share will make life with twins easier for you.

It's no secret that raising two babies at once has its challenges, but try to brush away your fears and tune out the naysayers. Use this time to educate yourself and get your plan together. Whether or not you follow it to letter, you'll be able to draw on the tools, tips, and strategies in this book when you need them. Believe us when we say, you can two!

# 1

# You've Got This

When did you learn that you were expecting twins? Was it a welcomed announcement after months, or even years, of hormone injections? Or are you still trying to decipher what exactly the doctor meant by *two* heartbeats? Regardless of your current emotional state (which could be anything and everything), here you are. Maybe you're just settling into the first trimester, maybe you're rounding the corner toward the final countdown, or perhaps you've just brought your twins home and you're wondering, "Now what?" Well, let us be the first to tell you that parenting twins is a remarkable thing; you were made for this job and it is something you are specially equipped to handle.

## Congratulations, Seriously

There are two heartbeats, twenty fingers, and twenty toes. Whether or not it came as a complete shock, major congratulations are in order because you're expecting twins! There is nothing more wonderful than bringing a baby into the world, and you are doubly blessed. While you process the news and prepare for your growing family, remember this: There are many things to celebrate even if you're still not quite sure how you will function once your two babies arrive.

**You can handle it.** Maybe you were hoping to be twin parents or maybe you weren't, but there's a long line of twin parents who have done this before you, including us. Enjoying twin parenting is all about controlling what you can and rolling with what you can't. Your new mantra is "I've got this!"—tell this to yourself often, even if you don't quite believe it yet. Soon you will be double burping and changing diapers single-handedly like it's nobody's business. Strangers on the street will stop in awe of your new parenting super-powers, so own it.

**Built-in best friends.** The truth is that twins are ready-to-go playmates. They get each other in the most profound way. Although you will have to handle sibling squabbles like any other parent, you'll get a front row seat to the unique show and the privilege of watching their bond develop over the years.

**Special savings.** Many companies want to celebrate twin families with discount programs. Companies like Huggies, Luvs, and Pampers offer discount coupons for parents when you sign up for the multiple birth programs through their websites. Formula companies like Similac offer great vouchers that offset the cost of formula. While not all companies offer specific discount programs, in many cases, all you have to do is ask.

**For the experienced parent.** Already a parent, with two more on the way? Even better! This isn't your first rodeo. You have the foundational skills to more easily navigate the early weeks and months with twins. Welcoming twins into an established family creates the opportunity for everyone in the household to become leaders and helpers in their homes, especially young siblings.

If there is any apprehension in your bones, take a deep breath. We're here to help you reevaluate your perspective and recognize what a gift it is to be part of an awesomely special club.

## All Feelings Are Allowed

Finding out that you are expecting twins can generate a wide range of reactions. You might be all over the emotional map. You may land somewhere near elated and giddy, whereas your partner might be stopped at the intersection of "Oh crap" and "Holy hell." Wherever you may fall as you're reading this, it's okay. There is no right or wrong way to feel when it comes to learning that you are having two babies. It *is* a big deal. Allow yourself to feel whatever you feel without shame or guilt and certainly without any judgment. It's totally normal to question everything when you're faced with the unknown. Just remember that sometimes the best things in life take you completely by surprise.

Did your toddler or big kid take a Sharpie to the wall when you broke the news that they were now going to have *two* more siblings?

We aren't saying there won't be moments when your older kids tell you they wished the twins could be given back. Their own emotions will ebb and flow just like yours. Anytime you add another child or two into the mix, it's going to shake up the family dynamics, and there will be hiccups. Ride the wave and talk through it, even with little ones who might not understand in the moment. Do the best you can and have compassion for yourself, right along with your kids.

## More Than Just Surviving

The goal of this book isn't to tell you how to be a perfect parent, nor is this a survival guide. While there will be tough days, they won't all be tough, and we wrote this book to give you tips and techniques to confidently and enjoyably live life with two babies. People will tell you that all you have to do is survive the first year with twins, or that life as you know it is now over. We all know that adding a couple of babies to the family at once is life-changing. But in no way is it life-*ending*. Far from it!

We have combined our experience—our successes and failures—in parenting our own sets of twins and our conversations with parents all over the globe to give you actionable advice that you can use to plan and prepare. Our hope is that, with this book as a resource, you will embrace twin parenthood and thrive.

Don't be fooled by ideals of parenting perfection; every day with kids, whether you have one or 19, has its ups and downs. At some level, we all have to find a way to get through difficult moments, but we surely never need to settle for "survival" as the status quo.

# Single Parenting Twins

Learning that you are going to be a parent to twins can at times feel overwhelming for everyone involved. For those of you preparing to go at it as a single parent, leaning on those in your circle, accepting help when it is offered, and asking for help when it isn't directly offered will be especially important. Learn to understand your own limitations, but more important, accept that you can only do your best and that's it!

Think about specific friends and family members who will be readily available to help. Then decide to ask for help in certain areas. Based on the experiences of dozens of twin parents, here's what's most valuable for you to line up in advance:

+ Anytime call for help
+ Meal train
+ Laundry
+ Pet care
+ Grocery shopping
+ Bottle washing

Help like this is simple yet very useful in the first few months with twins, especially so for single parents, but it can also be a huge relief for couples if one parent has returned to work. Someone can stop by to watch the babies while you take a shower (or nap!); you can set up an online meal system so that willing people can bring you hot dinners or freezer meals; someone else can walk the dog, make a Target run, or wash a round of dirty bottles. Getting the help you need isn't usually a big memory in the making, but it is absolutely a small necessity that helps you get through each day.

# TWINCREDIBLE

*Barbara, mother of Doloran and Cooper (8 years)*

Having twins is amazing! The attention it brings makes me feel like I'm a little bit famous. When we travel, in particular, I see the curiosity and admiration of others. I cannot count how many times, after confirming that our boys are twins, I've watched the expression on someone's face change, followed by a comment about what a blessing twins are. I've also encountered so many others who have their own twins, as well, and love to acknowledge that to me. Our "twin club" is real and we are there to support one another, wherever we go.

# Finding Community

The saying *it takes a village* holds true for every parent, especially those of us raising twins. As parents, we need people in our corner who will celebrate our wins, troubleshoot our challenges, and pick us back up when things get tough. You may be an independent person who usually takes tasks on solo, doing so with ease, and if that is the case, more power to you! When your babies are born, though, you might want to shift your approach slightly. Parenting is naturally filled with some anxiety that comes with being responsible for the lives of tiny humans. Try to have at least one or two people in your circle who make you feel good, lift you up, and empathize with you, without judgment, when you share your latest parenting fail.

Consider adding a few parents of multiples to your growing circle of friends. Invest a little time seeking out even one other parent of multiples, as that is someone who will instantly empathize with your new situation. In all likelihood they have already been there, or perhaps they are right there with you, newly learning to navigate their family life. The truth is they need you as much as you need them. Why? Well, caring for two infants at a time has a very different set of challenges. Other twin parents will:

- Drop everything on a dime to come hold a baby, just to give your arms a break while you eat.

- Lend an ear at 3 a.m. to offer you support while you clean spit-up off your pajamas or commiserate with you on the days you never got around to brushing your teeth (sad but true).

- Celebrate the fact that one of your babies is sleeping through the night even though the other is still up every two hours. It sounds crazy, but that is a celebration that only twin parents can appreciate!

The value of building a community that surrounds you, cheers you on, and passes on an arsenal of baby gear is incalculable.

So how do you go about building a supportive community? We are not going to lie here; we found it bit awkward at first to actively seek out new friends, but everyone is in the same boat. Start by looking here:

1. Your local Parents of Multiples groups

2. Local MOPS (Mothers of Preschoolers, ages 0 to kindergarten) groups

3. Hospital parenting groups or classes, some of which are even geared toward twins

meghan
says

After the boys arrived, I immediately started going to a new moms' support group at the hospital. We'd meet weekly, weigh the babies, and feed. Not only did it feel great to get out of the house for a little bit, but to see that, yes, it wasn't just my boys who cried like crazy. I also felt really empowered being the only twin mom in the group. I realized I really was doing okay! Through that group I met some moms who asked me to join a new-mom exercise class. This was a game changer. We got personal training while our kids were cared for on-site. Yes, please! If there is a class in your neighborhood, give it a try. You never know who you'll meet.

# Let the Prep Begin

We didn't write this book to cover the fetal brain development of your growing babies, nor will we be making weekly comparisons between the sizes of your unborn children and fruit. We wrote this book to be a practical tool to use while you await the arrival of your twins.

We believe that education is empowering, which is the founding principal of our online community at TwoCameTrue.com. You can never be fully ready to become a parent, but some basic preparation before those little nuggets arrive will allow you to feel successful when that wonderful chaos comes knocking at your door. We want to help you enjoy those first few weeks and months with your babies by giving you some simple strategies to try with your twins when you are too exhausted to think. Ultimately, we don't want you to feel like you're struggling to survive.

The first few months with newborn twins are wonderful, exhausting, and yes, chaotic, too. So whether you and your partner are pregnant with twins, you're going to be single-handedly raising twins, you're expecting twins through surrogacy, or you're planning to adopt twins, you've come to the right place. Each chapter has been carefully designed with practical strategies to give you the fundamental information you need to troubleshoot nearly everything that arises *after* your babies arrive. This book is meant to be read before your twins arrive, so you have the opportunity to develop a plan. We want you to start your journey by confidently approaching the things that make parenting twins a bit more challenging, like managing the eating and sleeping of two babies. If you're only picking this book up after your twins have arrived, there's still plenty for you to benefit from as you dive into managing real life with multiples.

We added a little gift for you by reaching out to some of our favorite twin families. We asked them to share actionable tips that made life in their households a bit easier, as well as some feel-good stories to remind you that raising twins is something to celebrate.

# IT WORKED FOR US

*Stephanie and Stacy, parents of Joanna (6 years)*
*and Simon and Isaac (3 years)*

You've got this, but accept help. Recruit help. If you can afford it, pay for help. Stacy and I did some combination of all of those. Help may come from unexpected places. My father, a man who is a little rough around the edges (not exactly a "baby person"), helped us more than I ever could have imagined he would. Why? He was the only grandparent who was retired, so he was available. He couldn't change a diaper to save his life, and he wasn't going to help with household chores, but he loved our babies. I knew he was capable of holding one of the babies if both were crying, and I knew he could feed a baby a bottle. He did, and it saved my life! So know that you can do this—but also take help wherever you can find it!

We know that one book can't solve all your parenting challenges before you bring the babies home from the hospital. But when you're up to your knees in parenting multiples, sleep deprived, and slightly delirious, you will appreciate the time you took to read this book. Even if you abandon everything you planned, chances are your parenting toolbox will be full enough to help you know what to try next.

jenn
says

After struggling with infertility for three years, my husband and I were elated to learn we were expecting twins. We thought the best way to wrap our minds around their impending arrival was to reach out to other parents of twins . . . until we realized that we needed more resources than we had. This book is my attempt to prevent others from getting over-whelmed by the feelings of isolation and uncertainty that I felt. I hope you remember to look us up when you feel like life is a bit too chaotic and all you need is to connect with people who can relate.

# 2

# Preparing as a Team

Whether you're planning to parent as a couple or as a single parent with help from family and friends, success lies in your ability to get everyone on the same page. As you prepare for the arrival of your twins, it is very important to make a plan—whether or not you stick to it 100 percent—and make sure everyone involved understands and agrees to put in their very best and go "all in." It is impossible to achieve the same goal when you aren't a cohesive unit.

For both of us, the first trimester was a special time, filled with pure joy at the fact that we were having a baby . . . wait—we were having two! There is something exciting about keeping the rest of the world in the dark for a while, sharing the *best* secret with only your partner. It's an intimate time, and it doesn't last long. Before you know it, your belly will be expanding, inviting everyone around you to start asking questions and offering unsolicited advice.

Savor the privacy of what you're experiencing together. Be sure to share special moments with one another, start talking about your hopes and dreams as parents-to-be, and certainly start to discuss any worries. Having open conversations early on about the ideas you each have about parenthood is a powerful way to begin to develop a plan together. If you are already parents to another child, this will also be a time to reflect on your current family dynamic, evaluate what is working well, and determine where you need to make changes so that adding two more to your team can be a relatively seamless transition.

## Sharing the News

Your first order of business together is deciding when and how you want to share the news. Finding the perfect way to do so can truly test your emotions. If you have been waiting for a long time to get pregnant or you were blessed with this as a surprise, letting others know can be a nerve-racking decision for a variety of reasons.

Not everybody feels the same when it comes to announcing pregnancies, and the anticipated way friends and family may respond can

## Relationship 911

Reality check: Relationships are work! Even the best relationships hit bumps throughout the years. Bringing any number of
children into a relationship is a lot to handle, no doubt about
it. Add that to any existing difficulties in your relationship and
couples might not know where to turn or how to mend things.
Before you begin to focus entirely on your pregnancy and the
necessary preparations, proactively address problems you are
already facing. The first step in bolstering your relationship is to
reiterate your unwavering commitment to each other, reminding yourselves why you are together. When you can talk in a
supportive way about what isn't working and each be heard and
have your feelings considered, you will begin to lessen any distance between you. Then you can reestablish trust and support
in your relationship.

affect how parents choose to announce the news. Your partner might be
itching to shout it from the rooftops of social media. You might want to
wait until the news just can't be hidden any longer. Getting on the same
page about when and how to share is the first step. Deciding how to
process the responses you get is step two.

Be prepared for a wide variety of commentary. One of the reasons
we wanted to write this book is to counteract the negativity many twin
parents-to-be face when they share the news and receive less-than-
enthusiastic feedback. You are not alone if you have heard (or soon hear)
some version of these statements:

+ "Twins, huh? Wow. You're going to have your hands full."

+ "Double trouble, I'm so sorry!"

+ "One is hard enough. I don't know how you will do it with two."

+ "That was my worst nightmare."

+ "I feel so lucky to have dodged that bullet."

Most of us fear the unknown, so it's no wonder that these sorts of comments come from people who have no practical experience with twins. (Of course, some overly enthusiastic folks will want to tell you about their best friend's great-aunt's nephew who had twins, thinking that gives them some right to comment.) Don't let them undermine your excitement or your belief that you and you partner have every right to do a happy dance each time you think about your impending arrivals.

Going through fertility treatments can leave you feeling shortchanged when it comes to the traditional "finding out you're pregnant" moment. So, after a tough day at the fertility clinic with yet another setback, we decided to be spontaneous and find out the sex of our babies right then and there. We knew all of our embryos were the same sex so, no matter what, we were destined to have either boys or girls. The nurse whispered the sex of our children to my husband and he turned it into a really special moment for me later that day. He lined up three frames with photographs of loved ones inside, got flowers, and had a glass of wine waiting for me when I came downstairs. Before I saw what he had set out, he told me I needed to take a close look at the people in the photos. They shared something in common. After a quick glance, I got it: One day we would have boys! I started bawling. For us, the whole journey was anything but traditional. We decided to create moments for ourselves when we could—even through the hard times—that would help us write our own story.

# Benefits of the Team

All right folks, now that the cat is out of the bag, let the real preparation begin. Do you remember the moment you made that lifelong commitment to each other, staring into your partner's eyes? Now it's time to take a good hard look at each other once again and make some additional promises. When the going gets tough you can lean on the commitments you've made.

## Sharing Responsibility

Commit to sharing the responsibility. Making this commitment from the beginning holds both of you accountable. But it must be noted that sharing responsibilities doesn't always mean the workload will be equally balanced. Relationships are all about the give and take, including who can realistically handle what, when, and for how long.

The key is to divide and conquer the tasks. While one person might put cribs together, the other can wash and store all the sheets and baby clothes. Maybe one researches pediatricians and the other researches hospitals. While your partner is at a doctor's appointment, could you get the car seats safely installed? How the tasks are divided isn't important; it's finding the simplest and most efficient ways that you can both prepare.

## Communicating Regularly

Communication is the foundation of every great relationship. It also can be the first thing that breaks down. Before your life enters this new chapter, explicitly discuss how to keep the lines of communication open. An easy solution is to designate a specific and mutually convenient time of day to check in with each other. Dig deeper and offer more than a "Hey, how are you?" If both of you are exhausted to the core, use the time to brainstorm options for help that might allow you to catch more sleep here and there. If getting out of the house is a priority but seems impossible, map out a plan for getting out the next week, if not right away.

Before our babies arrived, we never had a formal discussion about communication with our husbands. But one encouraging compliment given in the middle of the night quickly turned into a daily routine that, to this day, keeps us connected with our husbands. You and your partner will face misunderstandings and frustration with each other—we all have—but don't let that prevent you from recognizing each other's good intentions and small wins.

It can be as simple as throwing up an air high five at 2 a.m. while complimenting your partner on how quickly he got Johnny back to sleep. Or maybe that steaming mug of coffee brought to you in bed deserves a really tight, extra-long hug of gratitude. It'll mean more than you know when you see a toothbrush laid out on the kitchen counter to gently remind you to brush your teeth, since you now forget to brush until after lunch. Simple gestures and encouragement build trust and open the lines of communication in the most profound way.

## Developing Trust

The rule in our homes is to always presume positive intent. *Period.* You are on the same team because you deliberately chose to be. When you find yourselves exhausted by trying to manage life with two newborns, you need to trust that words thrown around aren't intended to be hurtful. Sensitivities are heightened when you are hormonal, tired, and stressed.

Keeping that in mind, trust that *your partner always has your best interests at heart.* Write that down and put it in a place where you will see it daily. Nobody means to snap when exhaustion sets in, nor does anyone mean to hurt your feelings by questioning why you did something. Trust that your partner has your back. Let intimate connection help you hash out your disagreements, not bury or ignore them, and civilly return your focus to your new family.

## Working Off Each Other's Strengths

Without fail, one of you will be the more patient parent at 3 a.m., while the other won't be able to open their eyes before the sun comes up. Whatever the case may be, your strengths complement each other, balancing you as a parenting team. Capitalize on the fact that you are great at different things. Because you can't be good at everything, you will find yourself more appreciative of each other's efforts.

jenn
says

My husband had this incredible ability to get our babies back to sleep, especially in the wee hours of the night. I don't know what it was about him, but I swear as soon as he cradled them in his arms, they would pass out. I would end up pacing the hallway, bouncing and shushing for hours to get the same thing accomplished. So once I had a handle on the tandem feeding, we capitalized on his super strength at night. I got up, changed and fed the boys, and then my husband would magically swoop in and get them back in bed. Yes, we were both up at night, but the amount of time we spent dealing with feeding and getting them back down significantly improved when we tag teamed the nights in this way.

## Taking Things with a Grain of Salt

The spicy combination of hormones, stress, and exhaustion can take you both on a wacky rollercoaster ride. Words can be unintentionally misconstrued. Suddenly a harmless suggestion has become the reason why you're getting the silent treatment. In the heat of the moment, go back to the commitment that you made to be a cohesive team. When the dust settles, have an open discussion.

## Truly Letting Partners Help

Memes, GIFs, and online videos do a great job of helping us talk a big game with halfway witty posts complaining about the lack of help we get from our partners in the parenting department. The reality is, more often than not, we are actually unconsciously discrediting the work that is being done or even turning help away when it is offered.

When possible, parenting should be a partnership even when one person carries a heavier load. But if we unconsciously shrug off helpful offers, only adding more to our own plates, the partnership becomes unbalanced and frustration builds. Instead, be conscious of what your partner is offering and don't shy away from deliberately asking for help.

At times, it can be challenging to know what kind of help you need. During pregnancy and after, the simplest tasks can truly be the most helpful. When you're feeling overwhelmed, ask your partner to take a few minutes to research baby gear, come up with a list of hospitals to visit, throw in a load of laundry, run to the store to stock the refrigerator, or perhaps develop a simple household system that will keep you both organized.

# Common Concerns

What was the first concern that came to mind when you learned that you were expecting twins? "How will we afford two babies?" or "Great, now we have to move"? It is 100 percent natural to be initially flooded with concerns about how raising twins will impact your life. Bringing children into the picture *does* change things. Face your worries head-on, develop a plan to address them together, and then start digging into the fun stuff.

## The babies will be born too early.

This is a legitimate concern for *every* expectant twin parent. The best advice we can give you is to mentally prepare yourself for the possibility that your twins may spend time in the neonatal intensive care unit (NICU) and hope that it doesn't happen. According to the University of Rochester Medical Center, more than three in five sets of twins are preterm (born before 37 weeks). With that usually comes a NICU stay. Place your trust in the excellent medical team that you have selected to care for you and your babies and be prepared. Do the research early on to find hospitals in your area that are covered by your insurance with the best NICU care. Visit each one and decide where you both feel most comfortable. In chapter 4, we offer specifics on things to do to strengthen your confidence and minimize your fears.

## TWINCREDIBLE!

*Dana, mother of Easton and Lacy (3 years)*

Twins tend to make their own schedule, especially their arrival. When we welcomed our two at 35 weeks, we did not expect them to go to the NICU, but they did have to spend some time there. Whenever we were there, holding them both at the same time, they always found each other's hand. The NICU nurses told us that twins look out for each other.

## Twins will be twice as expensive.

Yes, twins are expensive, because *babies* (and the kids they grow into) are expensive. Think of it this way: If you were eventually planning to have more than one child, now you get to do it all at once. Sure, double the diapers and daycare for two is expensive, but remember that list you made of all those discount programs that are offered to families with multiples. While two children will always be more expensive than one, they won't necessarily be *twice* as expensive. Be diligent with your budget and smart about your spending.

## We won't have any time for our other child or children.

It may not be easy at first, but you can find time for your other child or children, and you will cherish those moments. You don't have to put aside long blocks of time or make elaborate plans. Spend 20 minutes working on a puzzle, playing with Hot Wheels tracks, or just reading books. Try taking a quick trip to the park with some ice cream or getting out of the house 10 minutes earlier to grab donuts before preschool drop-off. Time away from your newborn babies is not only healthy but refreshing, too. You can find small moments in each day, such as when the babies nap, to devote to your other children, focusing your energy on the quality of the time you have together. Be it five minutes or two hours, your children will appreciate the time spent with them—even if they never acknowledge it.

## We won't have any time for each other.

You are about to enter a season of life that will require your attention to shift for a bit, but it's not permanent. Your relationship will change as you adjust to your new life, but it will also flourish immensely as you watch each other discover who you are as parents.

The way you honor your relationship and make time for each other may look different as your family grows. Your Friday night dinner date may turn into pizza on the couch, and that's okay. What matters is what you do with the time that you have together. Maybe one night instantly turning on Netflix is exactly what you both need. Another night, make time for a meaningful conversation over a glass of wine. Redefine what time together means and what it looks like as well.

When friends and family offer to babysit, even if it's only for an hour, take it and *run*! Head out for a quick date ... even if that means you're eating dinner at 4:30 p.m.

## IT WORKED FOR US

*Chad and Jodie, parents of Charlie (7 years),*
*Hallie (5 years), and Jack and Luke (11 months)*

Our twins were our third and fourth children. We have dragged them everywhere with us, from school drop-offs and pick-ups to dance classes, volleyball practices, swim meets, and basketball games. They have had to go with the flow in terms of naps and routine, and it has taught them (and us) to be flexible. With our first child, we were all about routines and scheduling, and our son had a hard time if that schedule ever varied. There is no right way to do it but, as an experienced mom of twins who have older siblings, I can tell you that your twins will be okay if they're along for the ride! In fact, they love all of the activity and being part of the action, and they always manage to sneak in car or stroller naps on those crazy days.

## It will be hard to encourage individuality and give each baby enough attention.

You are having two babies at once, but they are unique people with two different personalities and different needs. You will quickly learn their individual cries and noises, as well as their quirks and nuances. Don't assume that what works for one will automatically work for the other. Instead, make a conscious effort to treat them as individuals by honoring their likes and dislikes or giving them choices (when they're older, and when it's appropriate).

As a couple, consider this: Will you call them "the twins," "the boys" or "the girls," or by their individual names? Will you dress them alike, in coordinating outfits, or in completely different ways? While it might seem arbitrary to talk about these things, these decisions can play a significant role in how your twins develop their own sense of self.

Although twins are born together, they don't always have to come as a package deal. When you're running errands over the weekend, it's okay to take one with you and leave the other at home with your partner.

## I won't be able to care for two babies by myself.

The great news is that you aren't the first and won't be the last parent in the world to have to figure this out. Yes, without a doubt, caring for multiple babies alone is a daunting prospect, but by no means is it impossible. While your partner is home post-birth—or while you have other support in the house with you—emulate what your day might be like when you are all alone caring for your twins. Begin going through the motions, with support at your side, so you can practice trouble-shooting any situation that may arise and work to build your confidence in caring for your babies while at home alone.

jenn
says

When the journey to start your family takes twists and turns away from a more conventional path, more people may be in the know. It was no secret to our family and many of our friends that we were struggling with infertility; we needed our people behind us. In fact, most people were so in tune to where we were in the process that they anxiously answered all of our phone calls, just hoping that we finally had news to share. We knew that once we did have news to share, it would be celebrated by all, but we felt a bit robbed of the traditional "ta-da, we're expecting" announcement. Once we knew that we were having two babies and that they were boys, we decided to give ourselves the gift of surprising our families with the names we had chosen and the meaning behind our decisions. Once we decided, on our own terms, to share names, we felt like we got back some of the celebration that we missed out on initially.

# Write, Write, Write

Communicating verbally isn't always the easiest or most effective way to express your feelings. Sometimes it is easier to write than talk. Jotting down a few ideas here and there can help put your mind at ease. You don't need to write a novel, but simply putting your words on paper can help you sleep a little easier at night. You could probably use that right about now! If you are thinking to yourself, "Hello, I cannot get excited about this. I am way too apprehensive and overwhelmed right now," try reading the next few chapters and then come back to this page.

## Journaling Opportunity

Do you lie in bed at night wondering who these kids are going to look and act like? What traits do you want them to acquire from you and what do you want them to gain from your partner, both physically and emotionally? Lift each other up here and brag a little. It's exciting to envision the best parts of each of you becoming a part of these tiny humans!

*I hope they have your . . .*

_____

_____

_____

_____

_____

Suggestions: compassion, goofiness, dimples, singing talent, determination, wit

## Journaling Opportunity

Use this opportunity to jot down a few thoughts about becoming parents of twins.

*What excites each of you about welcoming twins into your family?*

_____

_____

_____

_____

*What is the one hope you have for their future?*

_____

_____

*What makes you nervous about becoming a twin parent? Why? (Side note: If one of you isn't concerned about what's to come, that's okay, too! It's important to validate your partner's fears or lack thereof.)*

_____

_____

_____

*What are you excited to see your partner do as a parent?*

_____

_____

_____

# Mental Health Check

The first few days, weeks, and even months home with your twins will be both mentally and physically exhausting. Unless you've adopted or used a surrogate, someone in your partnership will be recovering from birth. Whether you are new to this experience or have been here before, know that hormones and lack of sleep can take their toll.

We found it extremely helpful to preemptively put some thought into how we would take care of ourselves, both individually and as a couple. Have you had an open conversation about any history of depression or anxiety? Although this is a sensitive subject, mental health can seriously impact parenting teams, thus making it imperative to talk about openly without feeling shamed or judged.

Every new parent wants to embark on parenting in a positive way. Do yourselves a favor and be honest with each other about any mental health history that needs to be addressed.

+ If postpartum depression arises after birth, how will you address it as a team?

+ What resources do you have to support your mental health needs pre- and post-birth? (see Resources, page 161, for some suggested organizations.)

+ Will you consider therapy and/or medication if suggested by a health provider?

Postpartum depression is a tricky thing that can't always be diagnosed with a checklist of symptoms. You might recognize that you're not feeling quite right, but really, you're not going to feel like yourself immediately after the babies are born, or even several weeks later. Women suffering from postpartum depression may exhibit constant, inconsolable crying, have trouble bonding with their babies, struggle with sleeping and eating, or even seem disconnected from everyone around them. Before birth, let those in your circle know about some of these symptoms, so that they may provide you support in getting help if necessary. At the same time, there is not one single set of symptoms that applies to all diagnoses, so if you experience any symptom that starts to concern you, seek help! Trust your gut.

Be prepared for some ups and downs. Know that you will have moments where you doubt everything, and that is *completely* normal. Every parent experiences doubts, whether they've just had one baby or two (or three or four or five!) There may be times when you do not feel much like yourself or you are struggling in your new role. If and when that happens, be sure to open up to those in your circle who are supportive and encouraging. There is nothing to be ashamed of or any reason to hide your emotions.

## Journaling Opportunity

While you are awaiting the arrival of your babies, use this opportunity to write down a few sentences to your future, postpartum self. Be sure to validate your anxieties and reignite your self-love. Make this a hopeful exercise that can help pull you out of any negative feelings.

*Dear future self . . .*

_____

_____

_____

_____

_____

Suggestions: I know you are exhausted and questioning all that you are doing, but give yourself some encouragement; you are doing a great job. You've got this!

# IT WORKED FOR US

*Amanda and Andy, parents of Bea (4 years)*
*and Perry Lou and Calvin (5 months)*

We heard from countless people that it was important to give our daughter plenty of individual attention after the twins arrived. While this is valuable and true, it's not always possible. With two needy newborns in the house, it was all hands on deck all the time. For the first month our normally happy daughter acted out—particularly when friends and family came to visit the new babies—which we interpreted as cries for our attention. However, when we eventually found the right way to talk to her about it, she told us that she wanted to help with the twins. She didn't feel like she was missing out on time with *us*; she felt excluded from the excitement with *them*. Whatever guilt we felt for our dwindling one-on-one time was quickly erased. She acted much better when we intentionally included her in day-to-day baby activities. Simple things like throwing away diapers, carrying bottles, letting her show the twins her books and toys, and holding them (with help, of course) gave her a sense of trust and responsibility that really helped with our transition to a family of five.

# In It Together Checklist

Although nine months can seem like an eternity, the truth is that pregnancy and preparing for your growing family can be a total whirlwind. We've created a simple checklist, broken down by trimester, to help you mentally and physically prepare to welcome twins into your lives.

## Trimester 1 (0–12 Weeks)

- ☐ Make promises to each other.
- ☐ Define preparation goals that you'll work on together.
- ☐ Define personal preparation goals that you would like your partner to be aware of.
- ☐ Consider how and when you'll share the news.
- ☐ Start thinking about nursery ideas.
- ☐ Find an obstetrician or midwife that you like and trust.
- ☐ Let your employer in on the news when you feel comfortable.

## Trimester 2 (13–26 Weeks)

- ☐ Register for baby gear (some you need two of and some you don't; see Essential Baby Gear, page 35). Do this early on!
- ☐ Seek out other twin parents and talk with as many as possible. Who did what before delivery? After?
- ☐ Develop a birth plan. Make sure to address preterm birth. This doesn't have to be elaborate, just an outline of what you want.
- ☐ Research pediatricians and hospitals with NICUs.
- ☐ Find and take birthing, infant-care, and parenting classes.
- ☐ Start getting the nursery together (paint, blinds, etc.).

- [ ] Have a baby shower.

- [ ] Organize and assemble gifts from said baby shower.

- [ ] Go on a date night. Your growing belly isn't too big yet and getting out feels great!

## Trimester 3 (26–38 Weeks)

- [ ] Tour pediatricians' offices and hospitals; finalize those decisions (around 26–28 weeks).

- [ ] Make sure your nursery is set up, with sheets and clothes washed.

- [ ] Pack a hospital bag around 30 weeks, just to be prepared (see page 58).

- [ ] Get the house ready for when you arrive back home.

- [ ] Have car seats professionally installed.

- [ ] Set up a phone or text tree and put someone in charge of it. This is a great way to spread the word, when you are ready, that your twins have arrived.

- [ ] Enjoy a few last pre-birth date nights.

# 3

# Gear and Other Essentials

The amount of gear that tiny humans require is mind blowing, and the short amount of time that the gear gets put to good use is even more baffling (hello, exersaucers, we're talking to you). The list of gear and essentials that you think you may need for your twins can easily feel overwhelming. Luckily for you, we have some good news. Although your family is growing by two, you won't need to invest in double the gear. Twins are two very different people who will have different needs and wants, likely at different times. This means that they probably won't be itching to sit in their swings and bouncers at the exact same time, so why have two of each? We learned from the mistakes that we made in our own stockpiles of somewhat unnecessary baby gear, so we can pass on this wisdom to other families expecting twins: There are actually very *few* essentials that you will need *two* of!

## The Big Picture

A fellow twin mom once shared some advice, reminding us that managing the day-to-day with two babies works rather smoothly when your living room is set up in a center-style rotation, mimicking, say, a kindergarten classroom. Being two former educators, this resonated with us and helped to guide what we bought for our babies and how we used it. Simply put, one bouncer, one swing, and one playmat can suffice for two babies. Just rotate your babies through each "station" when they want a change of scenery. Instead of spending the money on two of everything, spend the money to give yourself options, because the reality is not every baby is going to like the same apparatus. Think of it this way: If your babies cannot share something safely—car seats, cribs and mattresses, high chairs—you will need two; otherwise, trust us when we say less is definitely more.

Before you go scraping together every last penny to invest in the latest and greatest baby gear, remember that a well-thought-out baby registry, hand-me-downs, and garage sales are all great ways to stock up on the essentials.

# If You Already Have Kids

As a parent with other children at home, you are one step ahead and may actually have more things you can use with your twins than you might think. Let's take inventory, shall we? Logistically thinking through what you already have and how you may use it with two additional children is a valuable exercise to help you decide what else you will need. Remember that the purchases you ultimately need to make will depend on the ages of your other children when your twins are born. What are the older children still using, and what will your twins also require simultaneously?

**Strollers.** Does your child still ride in a stroller? If so, hang onto it. A single stroller can be useful when you want to venture out solo with your oldest child or even on a little date with one of your twins. If your oldest no longer rides in a stroller and you still have one, sell it and put that money toward a new ride. You will need a double stroller, so consider investing in a new one or a gently loved one. With many newer strollers, you have the option of adding a kickstand on the back so that an older child can stand and ride right along with the babies. Sure, you may feel like a traveling circus, but that's neither here nor there—you're all on the move together.

**Playards.** This will depend on how you use a playard. Is it simply a safe place to set your baby down while you cook or fold laundry? Or is it a place for babies to actually sleep? Depending on how you want the playard to function, you may want to add another one to your shopping list or registry. When our babies were super little, they often lay side-by-side in the playard. As they grew, however, they needed their own space, which shortened the usefulness of one playard for our families.

**Bouncers and swings.** Baby-soothing contraptions are a must, but there really isn't a reason to have two of the same! If you already have one, invest in another, but find something new and different. Why?

Not every baby will like the same thing. We found that our children took to every swing and bouncy apparatus differently. Having options helped immensely when we were trying to soothe two fussy babies at once. Your living room may resemble a baby Crossfit gym, with stations for everyone to rotate through, but we promise this will make it easier to keep everyone happy.

**High chairs.** Fortunately, high chairs or clip-on seats aren't something your new babies will use right away. You have five or six months to transition older children to big-kid seats at the table, seek out hand-me downs, or bite the bullet and buy another seat. If your older children will still need high chairs when your twins are around six months old, consider buying two more.

> *Space-saving suggestion. We fell in love with the lobster portable high chairs that fasten to the countertop. These allowed everyone to eat together at our bar-top counters without taking up a lot of space in our kitchens. Clean-up is easy as well because you can simply slip the covers off and toss them into the laundry.*

**Cribs.** Many families work to transition their older children out of cribs before new babies arrive, but by no means is that a must-do. In general, everyone needs their own sleeping space, so take a moment and make a plan as a family. Where do you want everyone to safely sleep? Once you have decided on sleeping arrangements for your older child, you can determine how many cribs you might need.

# IT WORKED FOR US

*Julia and Kyle, parents of Jackson and Luke (18 months)*

I breastfed for as long as I could, which was about three months. After that, for my sanity, we went to formula. My girlfriend gave me the best Christmas present I have ever received (well, besides my Christmas baby): the Baby Brezza Formula Pro dispenser. It is basically like a Keurig for baby bottles. This machine mixes the proper amount of formula with water and dispenses it into a bottle in seconds, literally. No more waiting or mixing. Push the button, choose the number of ounces to dispense, and voila! A bottle is ready to go at the right temperature.

# Essential Baby Gear

*"Do we really need two of everything?" "What essentials do we absolutely need?" "Please tell me what I can live without."*

We have fielded hundreds of questions like these from expectant twin parents. In combination with our own experiences, we know that parents want simple and straightforward guidance. Right away, we're going to discuss the items that you'll need two of, the ones you can live with just one of, and those that you really don't need at all. Following that, we've included a master checklist that breaks down all the baby gear essentials you potentially need, according to different spaces you may use in your home. Also included is a category for gear that parents use while out and about. Obviously, we created this checklist considering as many circumstances as we could possibly think of. So if something doesn't feel like it might fit into your lifestyle (for example, if you are exclusively formula feeding your babies) simply ignore our guidance in that area and move on. Our hope is that you can use our experience to rein in your anxiety in this department, do a little shopping, and move on to other preparations!

## You'll Definitely Need Two:

+ **Baby carriers.** Even if you purchase a twin carrier for wearing your babies, it is nice to have the option to allow someone else to wear one baby when you aren't alone.

+ **Nursing pillows.** Nursing pillows are great not only for positioning your babies securely for nursing but also for bottle feeding. Consider the Boppy brand so you and your partner (or anyone else) can feed the babies at the same time.

+ **Car seats.** If a car is your primary mode of transportation, there's no getting around the need for two car seats.

+ **Cribs and mattresses.** Though many babies don't start off sleeping in a crib as soon as they come home from the hospital, cribs are the safest sleeping option for your babies as they grow.

+ **High chairs.** There are lots of options when it comes to high chairs—some are freestanding, some attach to chairs or tables to save space—but having one for each baby, so they can eat at the same time, is key.

+ **Noise machines.** As we'll discuss later, white noise is incredibly helpful for infant sleep. We recommend having two machines, as you may need or decide to separate your babies for naps or sleep training.

## You Can Get Away with One:

+ Baby monitor with two cameras or a single wide-angle camera

+ Baby swing

+ Bouncer

+ Digital forehead thermometer

+ Infant bath tub, as it will be enough to bathe one twin at a time!

- Nail clippers

- NoseFrida, a tool for relieving your little one's nasal congestion

- Playard, such as a Pack 'n Play

- Playmat

- Twin Z nursing pillow, which allows you to nurse or bottle feed two babies at the same time

Keep in mind our recommendation to set up stations for the bouncer, playard, playmat, and swing, so that you keep the twins rotating through them without needing two of each.

## You Can Absolutely Live Without:

- **A bottle warmer.** If you have a Keurig, it dispenses a single serving of hot water at the perfect temperature to heat a bottle evenly (without hot spots). You can also use an instant hot water faucet if you have one.

- **A dishwasher sanitizing basket or bottle sterilizer.** Opt instead for the Medela microwave sanitizing bags, which we love.

- **A wipe warmer.** As we will talk about in chapter 6, don't create habits you aren't willing to maintain until your babies are out of diapers. In this case, what they don't know won't hurt them.

- **A baby food maker.** A steaming basket and a blender/food processor does the trick.

- **Baby hair brushes.** A fine-toothed plastic comb does wonders.

- **Crib bumpers.** Simpler is better here; infants should only sleep in their cribs with a sheet and swaddle or sleep sack.

- **Shopping cart covers.** There are sanitizing wipes for a reason.

- **An infant scale.** Do you want to make yourself crazy?

# The Babies' Bedroom

### One

- ☐ Changing table
- ☐ Changing pad
- ☐ Rocking chair
- ☐ Small lamp or night light
- ☐ White noise machine
- ☐ Bookshelf
- ☐ Side table
- ☐ Clock
- ☐ Thermometer
- ☐ Set of black-out shades
- ☐ Video monitor
- ☐ Hamper
- ☐ Dresser

### Two

- ☐ Cribs and mattresses
- ☐ Cameras for your video monitor
- ☐ Changing pad covers

### Three or More

- ☐ Waterproof mattress pads (4)
- ☐ Extra sheets (2–3 sets)
- ☐ Burp cloths
- ☐ Diapers and wipes
- ☐ Diaper cream, lotions
- ☐ Swaddles (don't go crazy here until you know what swaddle your babies like)
- ☐ Clothes
- ☐ Baskets and bins for organization
- ☐ Hangers for clothes in closets
- ☐ Pacifiers (optional)

# Your Bedroom

### One

- ☐ Breast pump
- ☐ Mini fridge (optional but can save you from running downstairs at 2 a.m.)
- ☐ White noise machine
- ☐ Diaper changing mat
- ☐ Diaper pail
- ☐ Large water bottle

### Two

- ☐ Certified safe sleep surfaces (bassinets, Dock-ATots, etc.)
- ☐ Pump part sets

### Three or More

- ☐ Burp cloths
- ☐ Diapers and wipes
- ☐ Pacifiers (optional)
- ☐ Extra pajamas
- ☐ Swaddles
- ☐ Bottles

# The Living Room

### One

- ☐ Playard to set babies down
- ☐ Swing or mamaRoo
- ☐ Exersaucer
- ☐ Playmat
- ☐ Diaper changing station
- ☐ Nursing station (snacks, water, meds from hospital, etc.)
- ☐ Twin Z pillow

### Two

- ☐ Nursing pillows (if you don't have a Twin Z pillow)

### Three or More

- ☐ Extra jammies
- ☐ Diapers and wipes
- ☐ Pacifiers (optional)

# Transportation and Outings

## One

- [ ] TwinGo carrier
- [ ] Double stroller or Snap-N-Go stroller to fit your infant car seats
- [ ] Nursing cover
- [ ] Diaper bag (backpacks are super useful)
- [ ] Trash can (for inside the car... trust us, you'll need it)
- [ ] Coffee shop gift card (leave in car glove compartment for when babies are napping and you need to take a long drive)

## Two

- [ ] Infant car seats
- [ ] Seat kick mats
- [ ] Car seat covers (double use for your nursing covers)
- [ ] Car seat cocoon for cold weather outings
- [ ] Car seat mirrors
- [ ] Single baby carriers (if you aren't comfortable wearing both babies simultaneously)

# Clothes and Toys

## Two

- [ ] Stuffed animals (lovies)
- [ ] Hospital outfits
- [ ] Swaddles (start simple here, you may discover that each baby has a different preference)

## Three or More

- [ ] Onesies
- [ ] Sleep sacks
- [ ] Washcloths and bath towels
- [ ] Pacifiers (optional)

# Set Up the Living Room

The fun of decorating a new baby's nursery is one of the best parts of those nine months when you're expecting, and thanks to websites like Pinterest, you can find lots of unique ways to perfect that space. But even though your nursery will be ready to host the babies when they arrive, you may be surprised by how little time you initially spend in there. There is a solid chance that the majority of your time will be spent in other parts of your house—especially the living room. We like to call these spaces "Nursery 2.0."

Adding baskets filled with feeding, nursing, and diapering supplies makes any room you may spend time in functional for new parents. When the going gets crazy—in other words, two babies crying simultaneously with messy diaper blowouts—chances are you'll have everything you need within reach so you can easily get everyone back to neutral. And don't forget mom! Have supplies nearby for the nursing mama, such as snacks, a water bottle, a breast pump, and the remote control.

Looking for another list because you can never be too prepared? Here's what to include in your living room baskets:

+ Diapers
+ Wipes
+ Portable, foldable changing pads
+ Diaper cream
+ Hand sanitizer
+ Water
+ Snacks (such as granola bars and beef jerky sticks)
+ Reading material (print or digital)
+ Remote control
+ Extra sets of baby clothes
+ Burp cloths
+ Swaddles or baby blankets
+ Bibs
+ Pacifiers (if using)

# Getting Real About Finances

Expecting twins can make you feel like you've won the lottery. When the time comes to pay for everything, however, it's a different story. Some couples will dive into preparations, filling their homes with all the baby gear imaginable. Others will need time to sort through their finances as they prepare for the impact two babies will have on their bank account. The financial demand that comes with bringing home two babies can be a source of stress, but thoughtful planning can help. It will put you in charge of your money, may ease some anxiety, and can set you up to secure financial stability for your babies.

## Financial Planning

Planning for the future can be done with honest and open dialogue between partners. Use this list to review your current financial status and to help you thoughtfully plan your future as parents.

TALK ABOUT YOUR FINANCES

+ Review your income, assets, and debt as a couple.

+ Renew your financial beliefs as a couple, making sure that you are on the same page.

+ Decide how you will manage your financial obligations. Who pays what, and how are your accounts organized (joint, separate, or a mixture)?

+ Look into costs of daycare or nannies, or consider the impact that giving up one income may have on your monthly budget.

# The Fun Stuff

Are you Team Theme or not so much? Maybe you have always imagined a perfectly crafted nursery theme like airplanes or ladybugs, or perhaps you are more inspired by a beautifully curated color palette. Decorating a room for your growing family is an opportunity to put your signature on this next stage of life. It is a fun and wonderful way to creatively prepare for your new adventure.

We had great fun with this part of our preparation. Spend time with your partner perusing your favorite spots to find unique decor, artwork, and books that add character to your nursery. If decorating isn't your cup of tea, you might try your hand at it anyway—you just never know what you will come up with. Or, if you are completely overwhelmed, this can be an excellent area to delegate to someone who would love to help out. Remember what we said in chapter 2? Practice communicating your needs and asking for help.

Truly, baby decor these days has come a long way from cutesy wall decals and musical mobiles. Not only has wallpaper recently made a comeback, but big box stores like Target have recently upped their game, too. The cribs, sheets, and room decor you can find nowadays are super versatile with a sophisticated and modern twist, keeping you from having to update your children's room every two years.

Are you rolling your eyes because you have other kiddos and you know you'll put this on the back burner for as long as possible? That's okay! There is a solid chance that no matter what your life looks like now, you're not going to bring home two cute babies with nowhere to put them. Have fun with this, but do what works best for your family.

## DIG INTO YOUR EXPENSES

+ Track your spending for three months.

+ Evaluate your expenses to determine areas of unnecessary spending. Eliminate these to begin saving for your growing family.

+ Build a nest egg of extra cash to help cover unexpected expenses before and after your babies are born (for example, the deductible for a NICU stay).

## DEVELOP A PLAN

+ Create a unified vision for how you want to pay off your debt and begin saving (if applicable).

+ Discuss your future employment. Will one of you stay at home? Is working from home and caring for your children simultaneously a feasible option?

+ List all possible child care options (daycare, family or friends, nanny, au pair) and their associated financial obligations. Are there opportunities for discounts?

+ If your household will have two working parents, sign up for a dependent care program, allowing you to take $5,000 from your pretax income for child care.

+ Think about education options for your children, such as private versus public school.

+ Research health insurance and factor in the added costs of having two more dependents on your plan.

+ Begin looking into any potential investments you'd like to make, 529 plans for college tuition, and a life insurance plan to secure your kids' financial future.

## UNDERSTAND WAYS TO SAVE

There are a multitude of ways that new parents can reduce the impact that children have on their finances. Financially caring for the needs of two babies at once doesn't necessarily have to be exponentially more stressful. Consider some of these money-saving strategies and how they may fit into your family lifestyle.

+ Breastfeed and/or pump breastmilk. If you are formula feeding, ask your doctor for samples!

+ Make your own baby food.

+ Buy and wash your own cloth diapers.

+ Look for essentials, gear, and clothing at second-hand stores.

+ Borrow what you can from family and friends. Bottles are a great thing to borrow from friends so you can find which brand your babies prefer. There is no need to waste money on a product that you won't end up using.

+ Look for social sites developed just for moms to find special savings and coupons (such as AmazonMoms.com and MoneySavingMom .com).

+ Purchase generic brands when available.

+ Use coupons and find discount programs especially for parents of multiples. Never hesitate to ask; some small businesses may offer you a discount. Similac and Pampers have great programs that send you coupons to help pay for formula and diapers.

+ Ask family or friends to babysit instead of hiring a sitter.

+ Prepare frozen meals so you have a fully stocked freezer instead of ordering takeout.

- Save any gift cards you receive rather than spending them right away. When things come up and you need to buy something for your babies, you'll have the gift cards to help reduce your out-of-pocket cost.

- Do some research before you buy. Target offers gift card incentives by giving you a $20 gift card for every $150 baby purchase. Stock up on diapers, wipes, and formula all in one trip to get that gift card. Then use that gift card toward your next baby purchase.

- Keep snacks on hand (in the diaper bag) and don't go to the store hungry—you'll end up buying way more than you need.

# TWINCREDIBLE

*Laura, mother of Cali and Gianna (18 months)*

There have been so many incredible moments I've shared with my twins, and yet it was hard for me to pinpoint this one until just the other day. We were in the car on our way home from the park, with music blasting. I sang and they giggled and mumbled words only they could understand. In that moment, I realized that I'd made it to the point where I could go out in public with them by myself, tackle all the challenges that come with having twins, and still be able to laugh and sing. I reveled in this sweet victory, and I know the twins sensed it, too. We have created the most incredible bond among the three of us. Of course, the giggles, sweet kisses, and instant eye contact when they're thinking the same thing are truly amazing, but what really makes this experience extraordinary is knowing we are capable of doing anything together.

# 4

# Delivery and
the Days After

One of the most anticipated days of your life can be when your children come into this world. We both remember feeling a bit nervous and anxious, but thanks to the time we took to prepare ourselves for that day, our excitement easily outweighed our nerves. You have likely thought a lot about the delivery, but maybe with some worried anticipation of what will actually happen. While there is no way to guarantee that childbirth will go exactly as planned, there is plenty that you can do to prepare for most circumstances. Ultimately, we all want to bring happy, healthy humans into the world. Before D-day arrives, arm yourself with knowledge. Your most powerful advocate is you; you are running the show and are in complete control here, but you can't push for what you want if you don't know your options.

# The Final Countdown

It's probably safe to say that by now you have revisited that intersection of shock—you know, the one where "Oh crap" and "Holy hell" meet. It's totally normal to be anxious as you near the big day. You *are* about to have *two* babies! Over the last six to seven months, the roller coaster of emotions may have taken you on quite a wild ride from shocked to settled to excited and right back to shock, with perhaps a dose of panic. As you near the end of this pregnancy, set aside that drive-through hot dog, stop folding onesies, and do some work to get yourself ready for the moment when you'll jump straight into twin parenthood.

## Create Your Birth Plan

When it was suggested to us that we create a birth plan (insert eye roll), we shrugged it off. But in reality, a birth plan contains much more than making requests like being fed frozen grapes through every contraction. Thank goodness we asked a million questions. Our births had a few different twists but, ultimately, we didn't feel too overwhelmed when things got off track because we were prepared for a multitude of scenarios.

Taking the time to develop a thoughtful birth plan can help ensure that your needs and wants are met during labor and delivery and that others caring for you thoroughly understand your wishes. Create your plan to help guide everyone toward the kind of birth that you hope for, but leave room for flexibility because you simply cannot predict everything that may happen. Be sure to define your preferences around the atmosphere in the delivery room and how you wish to be positioned, but remember that everything may change if need be. More important, consider the following questions:

+ Is a vaginal delivery on the table for you? You should know that your health and medical history will be the first determinants, followed (down the road) by the positions the babies are in.

+ If you are planning for a vaginal delivery, who do you want in the room with you? Do you plan to include additional family members, a doula, or maybe a photographer?

+ During labor, do you want to be able to move around freely to help ease labor pains? What, if any, laboring tools would you like to have available?

+ What, if anything, do you want to employ for pain relief? At what pain level do you anticipate wanting an epidural?

+ If you plan for, or in the event of, a cesarean, do you want to be able to see your babies' birth (with mirrors or a clear sheet)?

+ Do you want your partner to cut the umbilical cords?

+ Would you like your babies placed on your skin immediately after they are born?

+ In case of an emergency, who would you like notified?

+ Do you plan to breastfeed, formula feed, or use a combination of breast and formula?

- If you do plan to breastfeed, would you like the opportunity to breastfeed right away?

- Is it okay for hospital staff to offer pacifiers to your babies?

- Are you comfortable with your babies receiving eye antibiotics and a vitamin K injection after birth?

- If one or both babies need to be taken to the NICU, will your partner go with the babies or stay with you?

Use this list to figure out your game plan, but do not forget to communicate with your partner and professional caregivers. Remember, this is your time to huddle up and get the whole team on the same page.

## Choose a Doctor and Hospital

Let us reassure you that your choice in which medical professional cares for you during pregnancy is exactly that—your choice. Make sure that you have talked with them in depth about what you value in your medical care and what's important to you during delivery.

Making the decision about who your doctor will be and the medical practice you choose automatically narrows down your choice of hospitals because your obstetrician must have privileges to deliver at the hospital. Begin your research by finding the hospitals in your area that your doctor is associated with, and then consider the following about each facility. Don't forget to tour each option!

- How far would you have to travel from work or home?

- Is there a neonatal intensive care unit (NICU)? What level is the NICU? (See the next section for how to learn about and evaluate NICUs.)

- Is your insurance accepted?

- Some hospitals have religious affiliations. Is that important to you?

- What accommodations are available for your partner? Are private rooms an option?

## Learn About the NICU

The NICU is the Neonatal Intensive Care Unit in a hospital. These specialized areas of the hospital are equipped with highly trained nurses and doctors to support babies who need extra care. Typically, babies born prematurely spend time in the NICU, but there are cases when full-term babies need NICU care as well. There are four levels of the NICU and it's important to understand your options when you are considering hospitals for delivery and what that might mean should your babies be admitted.

**Level 1: basic newborn care.** These nurseries stabilize babies born full term or nearly full term.

**Level 2: advanced newborn care.** These facilities care for infants born at 32 weeks or later who need care for more serious conditions.

**Level 3: subspeciality newborn care.** These NICUs care for babies born at less than 32 weeks' gestation or with critical illnesses. Babies admitted to a level three NICU will have access to all pediatric subspecialities, including respiratory support.

**Level 4: highest level of neonatal care.** These nurseries provide the most acute care and are located in hospitals with pediatric surgeons and anesthesiologists. A level four NICU will facilitate transport to their hospitals.

As an expectant twin parent, it is imperative that you know if your preferred hospital has a NICU and understand what level of care it will provide should your twins need it. For your own peace of mind, we strongly suggest you only consider hospitals with NICU care available—that your insurance will cover, of course.

We make this suggestion for one reason: In the event that your babies need NICU care, you will want to be near them. If you deliver at a hospital without a NICU, the babies will need to be transferred and you will likely have to wait to be discharged to be an active part of their care.

# IT WORKED FOR US

*Naomi, mother of Harrison (4 years)*
*and Annika and Gaby (2 years)*

Our twin girls were born at 30 weeks and subsequently spent their first 40 days in the neonatal intensive care unit. The prospect of time in the NICU can be scary, but we are forever grateful for the care our premature infants received, as well as the positive edges in parenthood that NICU time afforded us. The nursing staff was consistent and strategic. Through their efforts, the girls were predictable in their feeding needs, and they learned how to put themselves to sleep from the beginning. By the time we went home, all we had to do was follow the schedule the girls were on and not introduce bad habits. Now, the girls can sleep through nearly anything. They had lights and beeping monitors and health care professionals poking at them on a 24-hour schedule for the first several weeks of life, so it's understandable that they can sleep through a little outside noise. Even though two years have passed, one twin can belt out a back-arching wail that wakes up everyone else in the house without disturbing the other twin, who is asleep only three feet away. After trying every sleep strategy with our older son, it has been an unexpected surprise not to dread bedtime struggles with our twins thanks to their NICU stay.

## Listen to Birth Stories

Millions of women have given birth and love to dish on their experience. Seek out birth stories from other women. Knowledge is empowering. You'll hear stories of births that went just as planned and other births that took a very unplanned turn. Hearing how parents reacted, redirected, and charted a path forward can be inspiring and helpful, even if the situations may seem alarming at face value. A friend of ours gave birth in a hospital lobby while her husband was getting their bag out of the Uber. Not exactly what they pictured, but hey, mom and baby were okay!

# Expecting Identical Twins

We talked to moms of identical twins and there was a recurring theme: They always just seemed to know who was who! So the great news is, chances are you won't get your babies confused as much as you think. Call it instinct, call it mom sense—whatever you call it doesn't matter—parents just know. Audible sounds, like cooing or crying, help new moms determine the difference between their identical twins in those first few weeks.

Julia, mother of identical twins, explained, "My husband and I both just had this instinct and knew who each of the babies were at all times. Physically, one of my sons had a much larger head than the other. In addition he had a birthmark that distinguished him. We didn't need to paint a toenail to mark them in any way, as we could easily tell who was who. However, our close family and friends had to ask us for ways to identify each baby. My mom stayed with us for a month and it was even hard for her to tell them apart!"

Are there things that make you particularly nervous about giving birth? We found great comfort in asking friends with twins about their experiences. Having someone's honest perspective is much more powerful than going into the whole thing blindly.

One of our favorite ways to educate ourselves about parenting is by listening to podcasts. Although they weren't super popular when we gave birth, they are today. When we need parenting advice or simply to feel understood, we turn to podcasts to get a real-world dose of motherly support. As you prepare for your twins' arrival and are looking to learn more about birth, consider starting with a few parenting podcasts.

# Is the NICU Inevitable?

Not necessarily. It all depends on the timing of your babies' arrival and how much they weigh. According to the nonprofit American Pregnancy Association, about 60 percent of twins are born preterm (before 37 weeks), with the average twin pregnancy lasting 36 weeks. On average, twins weigh around 5.5 pounds at the time of birth.

Having your babies stay in the NICU, be it for a few days, a few weeks, or even months, is emotionally and mentally challenging, there's no doubt about it. You can never be fully prepared to have to leave your babies at the hospital, but you should try to remember that NICU care is vitally important to their health. Be prepared for a wide range of possibilities such as leaving one baby and taking the other home, or having to leave both babies while you commute back to the hospital from home. And while it may not be how you pictured the start of your life with twins, having your babies in the NICU can have some practical benefits. For example, your babies come home already on a schedule, thanks to the NICU nurses.

We do want to remind you that you are the parent, thus you are in the driver's seat here. If one or both of your babies have a stay in the NICU, make sure your voice is heard with regard to the medical care they are receiving, and be sure that you are included in conversations about their care. Advocate for what you want and *always trust your gut*; there is no such thing as too many questions.

## Set Up Your Home

As we prepared for the arrival of our twins, Goodwill drop-offs happened weekly. We created laminated labels (with clear directions on how to wash and dry laundry) and attached them to every laundry basket in the house. And yes, we broke out the whiteboards. Do you see where we're going with this?

Decluttering, organizing, and purging (also known as nesting) are a natural part of preparing for new babies. Many pregnant women have a sudden urge to ensure their baby's (or babies'!) future environment is safe and secure. Not only do we want the nursery stocked and looking pristine, but we also want our homes, which always seem to be a work in progress, to be put together. Regardless of how early you begin nesting, it's probable that you'll feel like you are running out of time. Instead of panicking, prioritize! Here are some ideas for your nesting "to-do" list, but only if your heart desires:

**Prepare and stock your nursery.** Also create your living room baskets so they are ready for your arrival home.

**Give your house one last deep clean.** If you can, hire a cleaning service to take the load off your plate.

**Make labels.** Labels are extremely helpful, especially when people offer to help out in your home. Labels tell them exactly where you want things to be put away, saving you later frustration.

**Catch up on outstanding to-dos.** Are there certain chores, projects, or organizing goals you really want done before the babies arrive? List them and knock them out—or at least the ones that will really bother you if they're not done by the time the babies are born.

## Pack a Hospital Bag

Don't procrastinate like you did when packing for your last vacation. Pack your bag (or bags) long before you near the final hour, and remember to pack not only for yourself but for your partner and your babies. Make sure to install car seats in the car you plan to take to the hospital well in advance, too. Here are the hospital must-haves to help make a temporary home away from home.

FOR YOU

- [ ] Laboring supports like yoga balls or massage tools (check with your hospital to see what, if any, they provide)

- [ ] Toiletries: toothpaste, toothbrush, hair brush, hair ties, shampoo/conditioner, face wash, body soap, lotion, etc.

- [ ] Nursing tanks and/or bras

- [ ] Loose fitting dresses or pants with a stretch waistband

- [ ] Robe or loose cardigan

- [ ] Slippers or warm socks with grips (socks provided by the hospital aren't exactly cozy)

- [ ] Shower shoes

- [ ] Comfy going-home outfit

- [ ] Pajamas (2–3)

- [ ] Comfortable underwear (large granny panties, though the hospital will also provide mesh underwear)

- [ ] Bath towel (hospital towels tend to be rough and small)

- [ ] Snacks

- [ ] Breast pump and pump parts (While you will have access to a hospital-grade pump in the hospital, it can be helpful to bring your own so the lactation professionals can teach you how to use it)

- [ ] Eye mask to sleep (bright lights may flip on in the middle of the night when the nurses come in)

## FOR YOUR PARTNER

- ☐ Comfortable outfits
- ☐ Toiletries: toothbrush, toothpaste, deodorant, body wash, etc.
- ☐ Bath towel
- ☐ Pillow
- ☐ Extra sheet set or sleeping bag
- ☐ Shower shoes
- ☐ Pajamas (2–3)

## FOR THE BABIES

- ☐ Going-home outfits
- ☐ Important mementos (e.g., blankets crocheted by your grandma)
- ☐ Nursing pillows, such as a Boppy or a Twin Z pillow
- ☐ Pacifiers (if you plan to use)
- ☐ Burp cloths

## MISCELLANEOUS

- ☐ Camera with memory card and charger
- ☐ Electronics chargers (maybe include an extension cord)
- ☐ Cell phones
- ☐ ID
- ☐ Insurance card
- ☐ Prepared playlist and Bluetooth-enabled speaker
- ☐ Water bottles
- ☐ Gifts for nurses (optional)
- ☐ Extra bag for hospital swag

# TIPS FROM A PRO: THE NICU

*Sandi S. Gleim, BSN, RN, CCRN, and NICU Nurse*
*at Children's Hospital of Colorado*

As your NICU nurse, my priority is your babies, and their care is my primary responsibility. Your primary responsibility is to yourself and each other. This can be one of the hardest times of your life, and you will need each other for support. We want you to sleep (at home or in a hotel) feeling assured that your babies are stable. We will contact you concerning any changes. You need rest so you can have the energy and patience to learn all we are going to teach you. Ask family or friends to bring you meals, do your laundry, and take care of your home and animals. Designate one person to be your contact to the outside world so you can turn off your phone and focus on your babies.

It is important that you attend "rounds," when the team of doctors, nurses, nutritionists, pharmacists, and therapists caring for your babies discusses their progress each day. This is when you get updates about gestational age, weight, caloric intake, medications, upcoming tests, and other medical concerns. It is your opportunity to ask questions.

Bonding with your baby is vital. Your scent is very comforting, so take a small piece of clothing that has your scent and place it near your babies' heads; you'll see them respond to the smell. Both parents should do "kangaroo care" (skin-to-skin contact) as much as you can, holding each baby directly against your bare chest. Research shows that it is important to overall brain development.

Your NICU stay may be short or long, so take each day one at a time with the knowledge that you and your babies will be going home, and this NICU journey will be just part of your story.

## Plan for and Schedule Help

You may be the type of person who likes to do things independently, but there will come a time when you need to lean on your circle of family and friends. Well before your due date, and we mean *well before*, make a plan to have help available to you *while* you are delivering your twins, *while* you are in the hospital, and *when* you arrive home.

+ Ask your neighbors to feed your pets if you should go into labor suddenly.

+ Have your parents or a dear friend on call to pick up your other children from school when the time presents itself.

+ Are you the type of person who needs to spread the word to family and friends immediately? Don't take on this beast all by yourself. You'll have much bigger fish to fry that day. Put someone in charge of notifying your immediate family and friends with a text or e-mail chain.

+ Ask a close friend to make sure everything in your house is clean and ready for your arrival home.

It is important that everyone on your team knows their role when your babies decide to join the world. Having a plan in place, especially if your twins arrive early, will make the whole experience easier. No one wants to stress about logistics when your only focus should be bringing those babies safely into the world.

## Prepare Siblings

We've heard from countless clients that expectant parents of twins often feel more stress when they already have other children at home. It's a huge transition, not only for the entire family, but especially for your children. Change can cause anxiety in anyone, so we can surely empathize with our little ones as they get ready to be promoted to big brother or sister.

If anything, our number-one tip for parents is to *make your children feel special*. All they really want is to know that, although your family is expanding, they will continue to be loved endlessly! Reading books or having your other children take part in picking out something special for the new babies are great ways to include them in the preparations.

Kids will feel nervous because they don't know what to expect. Does anyone, really? You can be honest with them by sharing what makes you nervous about expecting two more babies, as well as what you are looking forward to. Laying it all out there for them, showing them that they aren't alone, also gives your children the opportunity to openly share their worries.

# They're Here!

Congratulations! Your babies have arrived and you're on the other side of some seriously hard work. Consider yourself a hero and take a prideful moment, because that's about all the time you'll have before someone needs to be fed or changed. In most cases, after about an hour of skin-to-skin bonding (if requested), some standard assessments will be performed for the health and well-being of your babies.

## Standard Procedures

Before delivery, consider how you feel about each of these being done, and specify in your birth plan if you'd prefer that some are not conducted.

**Weight and length.** As soon each baby is born, they'll be weighed and measured. Your partner may have a chance to be involved and even take a photo of these precious first moments.

**Apgar test.** This test is conducted immediately after birth to help determine if further medical care is needed based on how your babies look and sound. Your baby is scored from 1 to 10 in the areas of activity, pulse, grimace (reflexes), appearance (skin color), and respiration.

The higher the score, the better the baby is doing. Scores of 7, 8, or 9 are normal and indicate that the babies are doing fine. An observational score is given at one minute and five minutes after birth.

**Vitamin K injection.** This is given at birth to prevent bleeding, because babies aren't born with intact blood-clotting functions. Some families request to have this administered orally. Speak with your health care provider to discuss your options.

**Newborn screening.** This is a blood test administered by pricking the heel to test for multiple disorders, varying by state.

**Hepatitis vaccine.** This is now mandatory in most states. You can usually choose to administer this at birth or at the two-month check-up.

**Eye drops.** Eye drops are placed in the babies' eyes to prevent infection that could occur as a result of delivery (and which could cause blindness).

**Hearing assessment.** Many babies don't pass the hearing screening the first time. Don't be alarmed, as this is very common. It is a result of amniotic fluid being trapped in the ear drum, causing temporary hearing challenges.

# The First Few Days

Your babies' needs become your preoccupation from the moment they're born, and their primary need in the first few days is to be fed. They will sleep quite a bit, so grabbing moments for yourself to sleep between feedings and visits from medical staff will start right away. While we will take a deep dive in chapters 5 and 6 into all things related to the feeding and sleeping needs of two babies once you've returned home, in this chapter we cover what you can expect during your hospital stay.

# Delivery FAQ

Here are some of the most common questions that expectant parents ask us about delivering twins.

**WHAT IF MY TWINS ARRIVE EARLY? HOW DO I PREPARE?**

According to the University of Rochester Medical Center, more than three in five sets of twins are preterm (born before 37 weeks), so there's certainly a chance that yours will be, too. The best way to prepare is to be proactive and discuss with your doctor ways to maintain a healthy pregnancy. Second, you want to be sure that you understand the complications that can arise with a twin pregnancy and mentally prepare, just in case, for a NICU stay.

**WILL I HAVE TO HAVE A CESAREAN DELIVERY?**

Not necessarily. Consult with your doctor about your wishes and your health considerations, and prepare a birth plan that makes sense given both of these factors. While you may be told that it is unsafe to deliver twins vaginally if both babies are not in a head down position, research published in the *New England Journal of Medicine* in 2013 found that when twins were born between 32 and 38 weeks, and when the first baby had his or her head facing down toward the pelvis, there were no differences in the rates of fetal death or serious complications between one group of women who'd planned to deliver vaginally and another group of women who had planned cesareans. If you feel strongly about delivering vaginally, you may want to explore all of your options when it comes to a selecting an obstetrician.

**IF MY BABIES NEED TO STAY IN THE NICU, CAN I STAY TOO OR DO I GO HOME?**

This is highly dependent on the hospital where you deliver or where your twins are transferred to. In our experience, few

NICUs have the ability to provide lodging accommodations for parents. You can go home and commute back and forth or find a nearby hotel or Ronald McDonald House to stay at until your babies are discharged.

**WHAT ARE MY CHANCES OF HAVING ONE BABY VAGINALLY AND THE OTHER NEEDING AN EMERGENCY CESAREAN?**

This is quite rare. Typically, this happens due to complications like a cord prolapse, malpresentation (that cannot be moved) with Baby B, or a placental abruption, in which the placenta tears away from the uterine wall prematurely.

**WHAT WILL RECOVERY FROM BIRTH LOOK LIKE FOR ME?**

Your recovery will depend on your labor and delivery. Recovering from a vaginal delivery will be different than recovering from a cesarean delivery. Having a cesarean will limit your ability to lift anything or drive for about two weeks after birth. Bleeding and discomfort will usually subside within six weeks. Icing and soaking your lady parts or using witch hazel are great ways to relieve those pesky postpartum discomforts (yes, like hemorrhoids!).

**HOW CAN I CURB THE MOM GUILT FOR NOT BEING ABLE TO PLAY WITH MY OTHER CHILDREN RIGHT AWAY?**

This is a tricky one. As a parent, you want so much to be with your other children, but in reality, your new babies initially will likely consume the majority of your time. The good news is that newborn babies sleep a lot. Capitalize on their sleepiness by spending time with your other children. Sneaking in a quick trip to the park, playing a board game, or grabbing some ice cream can alleviate some of the guilt and even help your children adjust to the new family dynamic. No matter which way you play it, you'll probably feel some guilt. It's hard, but hang in there! Know that you are doing your best and that is all anyone can expect.

## Feeding Expectations

Newborn babies eat *a lot.* They may start out feeding around the clock, but within a few days after birth they will develop more of a pattern, wanting to eat about every two or three hours. At birth, a newborn's stomach is the size of a cherry and grows to be about the size of a large egg by the end of the first month. This means that they will eat 1 to 1.5 teaspoons per feeding the first day of life, ¾ ounce by day three, 1.5 to 2 ounces by day seven, and 2.5 to 5 ounces by the end of the first month. Take a look at one of those baby bottles you've purchased—1 ounce is not very much at all!

The best advice we can give you is to work closely with the hospital's lactation consultants for breastfeeding support. A lactation consultant is a board-certified professional who supports mothers in the management of breastfeeding and lactation. The nurses or pediatrician can assist you with any formula feeding or supplemental needs while you are in the hospital.

## Breastfeeding

If you have never had a baby before, there can be quite a bit to learn when it comes to breastfeeding. While breastfeeding is often described as the most natural of acts between a mother and baby (or babies), *natural* doesn't mean it will happen quickly or easily. There can be a learning curve, particularly with twins, and there's a vocabulary that goes along with the breastfeeding endeavor. Here are some terms you may hear in the hospital, including things you can expect in the first few days when it comes to breastfeeding.

**Areola:** The pigmented area around your nipples. During pregnancy, your areolas darken, which is your body's mechanism to help babies more easily find your nipples.

**Rooting:** This is a normal reflex in babies looking for food. They will turn toward a stimulus and begin making sucking motions when you touch their cheeks or lips.

**Latch:** A good latch is essential to successful breastfeeding. In order to have a sustainable latch that works for you both, you want to be sure your baby's mouth has a good seal around the nipple and that you aren't experiencing any pain.

**Colostrum:** This yellowish, creamy, nutrient-rich substance is your babies' first food and is produced by your breasts for the first three to four days postpartum.

**Foremilk:** Foremilk is the first milk released from the nipple during a feeding. It has a watery consistency that quenches your babies' thirst.

**Hindmilk:** Hindmilk comes after your milk is flowing substantially, much like dessert. This milk is creamier and has a higher fat content. Your babies get most of their calories from hindmilk.

**Engorgement:** This describes overly full breasts. They will feel hard and swollen, and it will be harder for your babies to breastfeed.

**Let down:** Let down occurs when a mother's body receives signals (from her babies sucking on the nipple) to release milk. It can feel like pins and needles as the milk works its way from the ducts. (While breastfeeding, don't be surprised if any discomfort from your uterus contracting to get back to its original size is slightly more intense.)

**Lanolin:** This ointment, extracted from sheep's wool, helps moisturize, heal, and soothe sore or cracked nipples.

In the first few days after birth, your milk will change from colostrum to mature milk (a thinner, white fluid). This change typically occurs between 48 and 72 hours after birth, although it can take a little longer following cesarean births. During a feeding, your milk will also change, starting off as a more watery liquid and changing to a fattier substance as the babies eat. Letting your babies feed on one breast as long as they want will ensure that they are getting the calories and nutrients that they need.

Breastfeeding can be tough for some women, especially those trying to feed two babies at once. Get as much help as you can before you are discharged, and before you head home, make arrangements to have support, be it weekly appointments with a lactation consultant or breastfeeding support groups. Having resources and support by your side are powerful tools for breastfeeding success.

## Sleeping Expectations

Eat, sleep, poop, repeat! This is the life of a newborn. In the beginning, babies sleep *a lot*. In fact, they will spend more time asleep than they will awake, sleeping 14 to 18 hours in a 24-hour period up until six weeks or so.

## Your Hospital Stay

This may seem counterintuitive, but try to stay in the hospital for as long as your insurance allows. In the hospital, you are surrounded by professional support during those first few days when you are trying to get to know your new babies and their needs. Recovering from birth, especially if you had surgery, is no walk in the park. Being cared for by medical professionals is really helpful. You might feel keen to get home, but take it slow and get as much help from the hospital staff as you can.

When it's time for you to go home, take (almost) everything from your hospital room. Get out the extra bag you brought (from the packing list, page 58) and start filling it with the supplies that are brought to your room each day. Take the diapers, wipes, snot suckers, pacifiers, swaddle blankets, pee pads, and whatever else you are given. Both of us were more than happy to take home our amazing double-insulated hospital water bottles. Your hospital stay costs whatever it costs whether you use 5 diapers or 100. Take the swag! You can always donate what you don't use.

# Before Leaving the Hospital

☐ **Have your baby exam.** A pediatrician will examine babies and administer the heel stick blood test to screen for metabolic disorders.

☐ **Have your mother exam.** Doctors will check that you are beginning to heal properly, your uterus is contracting, and your bleeding is slowing.

☐ **Have your skills check.** Hospital staff will ensure that your babies are successfully breast or bottle feeding and you understand bathing, cord care, and diapering.

☐ **Make sure your car seats are properly installed.** Many hospitals have certified staff members who can check the car seat installation.

☐ **Check that you have:**
  - ☐ *Birth certificates/Social Security paperwork*
  - ☐ *Discharge instructions*
  - ☐ *Gift from visitors—cards, flowers, balloons, etc.*
  - ☐ *Your bags packed*

☐ **Take any photos you want:**
  - ☐ *First bath*
  - ☐ *In bassinet*
  - ☐ *Meeting siblings*
  - ☐ *As a family; just with each partner*
  - ☐ *Going-home outfit*
  - ☐ *Going home*

☐ **Make follow-up appointments.** One appointment needs to be with your pediatrician (for babies) and the other with your obstetrician (for mom). Mom needs to see her doctor six weeks after birth, unless otherwise instructed. The babies need to be seen 48 to 72 hours after discharge.

☐ **Load up on the free stuff.** Take things like diapers, wipes, formula, and donor milk.

☐ **Ask for information on resources to support you once you are at home.** These are things like a lactation consultation or a new moms' baby group at the hospital.

# TWINCREDIBLE

*Ozzie and Bart, parents of Nadia Grace and Jacob Felix (16 months)*

Our twins were delivered via surrogacy in a neighboring state approximately four hours from our home. Once we received the call, we hauled it out of town knowing there was a chance we would miss the delivery of our twins. Luckily, we made it to the hospital with time to spare. We had planned for this day for so long, toting our laminated birth plan in our back pockets, but it felt as if we knew nothing!

The twins were born healthy and full-term which meant we could leave the hospital 24 hours after they were born. We couldn't believe we'd just become parents and were leaving the hospital with no parenting manual! But here we are with 16-month-old twins. We may be more tired than we used to be, but we still manage to high-five each other every night without fail. We now know that we can get through anything!

# Life at Home

With delivery behind you, it's time to go home. Wait. Back up a minute. Before you leave the hospital, be sure to discuss and arrange what you want when you arrive home. Who, if anyone, do you want there to welcome you? Do you want Uncle Eddie and his RV parked on the street when you show up with two new babies? Do you want people coming by to drop off meals for you? What will you want to eat? Have you had a crazy craving the past few months? Make the dream come true. You deserve it, so ask for it, and plan for it. We often suggest that expectant twin families have a deliberate conversation about this moment so the transition home can go smoothly while you begin adjusting to your new normal.

At home, your main priority should be settling into your new life. Take it slow, and keep your expectations realistic. Remember, one of you is likely recovering from birth and hormones are trying to readjust. Ups and downs are *completely* normal, as are a few living room scuffles. Be patient with each other and lean on that conversation you had, pre-babies, about mental health (see page 25).

People will be chomping at the bit to see your babies, but you don't have to have everyone you know stopping by in the first few days if that will overwhelm you. Give yourself permission to allow visitors as you are comfortable, ask them to stay away if they might be sick, and always have them wash their hands before they hold the babies.

Have you ever considered calling the doctor because of a weird sneeze? Wait until you have two newborn babies living with you. You can and likely will want to call the pediatrician, often, with many questions. You might feel reluctant to keep bothering them, but they truly would rather you do that than worry unnecessarily. When in doubt or when you see a change that concerns you, call the doctor. It's what they are there for.

## Schedule Tracking

Juggle two babies and add in a hefty dose of sleep deprivation and it's entirely possible that you might find it hard to keep track of everyone's needs. Doubt that you will ever change the same baby's diaper twice instead of giving each twin a change? It'll happen! It's certainly not necessary, but if you think it would help you, consider using a schedule tracker. After all, in the hospital each baby's diaper changes (and whether they were pee diapers or poop diapers) and feedings were tracked. It makes sense to do it at home, especially since your pediatrician will also want you to share this information.

A schedule tracker is a great tool for parents juggling multiple children because they help keep all caretakers (grandparents, friends, postpartum doulas, etc.) on the same page and will definitely save you a pointless diaper change or two. On the next page is a sample of everything that should be captured in a schedule tracker for each twin. The good news is that we've created sample pages for Baby A and Baby B, and you can download them at CallistoMediaBooks.com/YouCanTwo. Print out 150 copies (yes, you heard us right!), punch a hole in them, and put them in a binder. Don't forget the pen or pencil.

## IT WORKED FOR US

*Jill and John, parents of Harper and Hannah (4 years)*

Our girls were born early and had to stay in the NICU for a couple of weeks. I had already spent the previous five weeks in the hospital due to complications related to preeclampsia. After such a prolonged stay, my hospital room had become our second home. We even had a Christmas tree! After the girls were born, the hospital rented us the room for two weeks until the girls were released from the NICU. Although I was so tired of being at the hospital, it was a blessing not to have to drive back and forth from home several times a day. I was able to recover from my cesarean, all while being right down the hall from my girls. Check with your hospital to find out what additional services they might have available to make your stay more comfortable and convenient.

# TWIN SCHEDULE TRACKER

Day/date: _____

## Baby A:

| TIME | FEEDING | DIAPER |
|------|---------|--------|
|  | ___ mins / ___ounces | bm ___ pee ___ |
|  | ___ mins / ___ounces | bm ___ pee ___ |
|  | ___ mins / ___ounces | bm ___ pee ___ |
|  | ___ mins / ___ounces | bm ___ pee ___ |
|  | ___ mins / ___ounces | bm ___ pee ___ |
|  | ___ mins / ___ounces | bm ___ pee ___ |
|  | ___ mins / ___ounces | bm ___ pee ___ |

| SLEEP TIME | DURATION | NOTES |
|------------|----------|-------|
|  |  |  |
|  |  |  |
|  |  |  |
|  |  |  |
|  |  |  |
|  |  |  |

# 5

# Feeding

We wish we could tell you that feeding two babies is as simple as latching them to a breast or putting a bottle in their mouths. For some that may be the case, but for most parents, successfully feeding their babies requires some education and support. Let us reassure you, as two moms with thriving toddler and kindergarten-age twins, if we can do this, you can, too.

This chapter is all about the realities of feeding two babies, whether you're doing so via breast, bottle, or a combination. We've tried to incorporate all the tips and tricks we've learned through our experiences and others' that might help you troubleshoot if feeding becomes challenging. We were both once there, doing our best to feed two babies, only we were much less prepared then than we are now. How you decide to feed is entirely your choice based on what works best for your babies, your lifestyle, and your family. There really is a way for every parent to successfully feed two babies when you approach the whole endeavor with the mind-set that "fed is best."

# Feeding Needs

For singletons or twins, breast or bottle, the general rules for feeding a baby apply to all. The first step to feeling successful in the feeding department is to have a basic understanding of nutritional needs as babies grow and develop throughout their first year of life. Keep in mind that it is normal and *expected* for babies to lose weight immediately after birth, so don't worry when yours do; it isn't necessarily a sign of them being underfed or sick.

## How Much Should Babies Eat?

This is one of the most common questions we hear, and we, too, struggled to understand how much to feed newborn babies. Infants' bodies are growing and changing rapidly, making it hard for parents to feel confident that they are getting feedings right. Babies eat often because they are born with stomachs the size of cherries, but by the third day of life, their stomachs have grown to about the size of walnuts. Even in three days, the amount a baby needs at each feeding has changed dramatically. The chart we put together (page 78) will give you an at-a-glance guideline for the amount of food babies are capable of eating at certain age milestones, as well as expectations for diaper changes.

## How Often Should Babies Eat?

For the first few weeks of life, babies will eat every one to three hours, translating into 8 to 12 feedings a day. As with everything, these are approximations and will depend on your individual children, but this schedule should help you get a feel for what your days may look like as your babies grow.

## Understanding Hunger Cues

Ever smell a piece of pizza and feel like you could take a bite off a stranger's plate? You probably missed your own hunger cues and are hangry! Most of us would assume that infants are hungry when they begin to cry, but the truth is that crying is actually a late hunger cue. When babies first feel hungry they will begin to stir or smack their lips together, open their mouth and begin rooting (seeking food), and suck on anything that is nearby. Being cognizant of these early hunger cues and promptly feeding your baby will usually result in a successful feeding. As your babies get hungrier they will become extremely fidgety and fussy, often putting their hands in their mouths. Once they are *really* hungry, they will become agitated, turn red, and begin screaming and thrashing from side to side. Understanding your babies' hunger cues will ultimately help you develop a stronger feeding relationship with your infants.

# Feeding and Elimination Expectations by Age

| | 1 DAY OLD | 3 DAYS OLD |
|---|---|---|
| **SIZE OF BABY'S STOMACH** | Cherry | Walnut |
| **BREASTMILK OR FORMULA** | 1 to 1.5 teaspoons (5 to 7 ml) | 0.75 to 1 ounce (22 to 27 ml) |
| **PEE** | At least 1 or 2 wet diapers | At least 3 wet diapers |
| **POOP** | At least 1 or 2 dark black/green poops per day | At least 3 brown/green/yellow poops per day |

## Feeding on Demand versus on a Schedule

One piece of advice that you will hear from us, over and over, is to try and do everything for your babies at the same time. This will keep your life more manageable. While we don't want to discredit some of the benefits of feeding on demand, trying to feed two babies this way will naturally be time consuming and potentially overwhelm your day with feedings. With that being said, you will likely start out feeding on demand until you get the hang of being a parent of twins who need to eat nonstop. For the first six weeks or so, pay close attention to patterns that begin to develop and use those as a guideline to begin implementing a more scheduled approach that works for your family.

| 1 WEEK OLD | 2 WEEKS OLD | 6 MONTHS TO 1 YEAR OLD |
|---|---|---|
| Apricot | Large egg | Grapefruit |
| 1.5 to 2 ounces (45 to 60 ml) | 2.5 to 5 ounces (80 to 150 ml) | 6 ounces to 2 cups (180 ml to 0.4 L) |
| At least 6 wet diapers | | |
| At least 3 soft, seedy, yellow poops per day | | At least 1 large, yellow poop per day (although every 1 to 7 days can be normal) |

## A Word About Reflux

We wouldn't be doing our jobs if we wrote an entire chapter about feeding your new infants without saying something about reflux. Why? Well, it impacted both of our families pretty profoundly, and initially we didn't feel equipped to deal with it or even really know what it was. *USA Today* claims that reflux (gastroesophageal reflux or GER) occurs in 25 percent of babies to some degree and can result in symptoms ranging from frequent spitting up to more severe colic-like conditions with abdominal pains and night wakings. Always communicate with your doctor. If you are looking for a community, you can connect with other parents whose children had reflux by visiting the Pediatric/Adolescent Gastroesophageal Reflux Association (www.reflux.org.au).

# Feeding Schedules by Age

| 0 TO 3 MONTHS | | 3 TO 6 MONTHS | |
|---|---|---|---|
| **WAKE TIME** | | **WAKE TIME** | |
| **45–60 MINS** | | **1.5–2 HOURS** | |
| 7 a.m. | Wake/Feed | 7 a.m. | Wake/Feed |
| 8 a.m. | Nap | 9 a.m. | Nap |
| 9–10 a.m. | Feed | 11 a.m. | Feed |
| 11 a.m. | Nap | 12 p.m. | Nap |
| 12–1 p.m. | Feed | 3 p.m. | Feed |
| 2–4 p.m. | Nap | Between 3:30–5 p.m. | Nap |
| 4 p.m. | Feed | 6:30 p.m. | Feed |
| 5–6:30 p.m. | Nap | 6:45 p.m. | Bed Routine |
| 6:30 p.m. | Feed | 7 p.m. | Lights Out |
| 7:30 p.m. | Nap | | |
| 9 p.m. | Bed Routine | | |
| 9:30 p.m. | Lights Out | | |

| 6 TO 9 MONTHS | | 9 TO 12 MONTHS | |
|---|---|---|---|
| **WAKE TIME** | | **WAKE TIME** | |
| **2–3 HOURS** | | **3–4 HOURS** | |
| 7 a.m. | Wake/Feed | 7 a.m. | Wake/Feed |
| between 9–10 a.m. | Nap | 10 a.m. | Nap |
| 11 a.m. | Feed | 11 a.m. | Feed |
| 12:30 p.m. | Lunch (solids) | 12:30 p.m. | Lunch (solids) |
| 2 p.m. | Nap | 2 p.m. | Nap |
| 3 p.m. | Feed | 3–3:30 p.m. | Feed |
| 5:30 p.m. | Dinner (solids) | 5:30 p.m. | Dinner (solids) |
| 6:30 p.m. | Bed Routine* | 6:30 p.m. | Bed Routine* |
| 7 p.m. | Lights Out | 7 p.m. | Lights Out |

*Your bedtime routine should include the final feeding for the day.*

While you can't make the discomfort of reflux completely disappear, there are some simple things you can do to help make your babies more comfortable:

+ Keep babies upright for 15 to 30 minutes after a feeding.

+ Offer smaller, more frequent feedings.

+ If formula feeding, use a hypoallergenic or gentle stomach formula.

+ Elevate your babies' heads while they are sleeping.

## TIPS FROM A PRO: PREPARING TO BREASTFEED

*Stephanie Moore, RN, BSN, IBCLC*

Why not consider breastfeeding like you would a loosely planned excursion? Reservations are made, vacation time is scheduled, wardrobes are planned and, as expectant parents, cancellation insurance has been purchased. There's no getting around that life has a way of just happening! With breastfeeding, mom is learning how to physically breastfeed two infants, each with a unique feeding style. Sometimes feeding plans go as planned and other times a detour is necessary to get to the destination. Go on this journey together. Some things will come easy for mom, for one baby, for both babies, or for neither. That is okay. Mom learns the mechanics and her partner and other close support people give her the confidence to do the learning. Just like when visiting a new city, when alone one might not venture far from home base, but with a trusted companion one is more confident exploring the city and having new experiences.

Breastfeeding is just like that. Preparation is in place, support people are your companions, and lactation professionals, your guides. The babies will teach you what you need to know about breastfeeding. It is only when the babies are in your arms and are nestling to be fed that breastfeeding starts to make sense.

# Breastfeeding

Breastfeeding is wonderful for many reasons, but speaking from experience, it doesn't always come easily. From how your breasts fit with the babies' mouths, to your milk supply, to the particular issues you encounter, breastfeeding varies from person to person. However, as we have said before, knowledge is empowering. Before your twins arrive, soak it all in and ask questions of people who have been there before. Remember to be patient with yourself while you get a little experience under your belt. It's *not* easy for everyone, even if your best friend tells you she breastfed with no hands, upside down, and with enough milk flowing for 12 babies. Some women love breastfeeding, some despise it, and some would love to do it but just can't. *Wherever you fall, do what is best for you!*

## From the Start

If you plan to breastfeed, talk with your obstetrician before delivery about your goals. Together you can make a plan that will support your desire to breastfeed immediately after birth. It is important that the nipples get stimulated soon after birth to establish your milk supply.

## Get Help

From the moment you decide to breastfeed, even before your babies are earthside, get help. Take advantage of the support while in the hospital, but then find a certified lactation expert who can support you once you are home. Be sure that the person you entrust looks at the mom-baby duo when helping you troubleshoot. For instance, it is important to look at how the baby's mouth and the mom's nipple work together when trying to solve any breastfeeding problems that may arise.

When you start out breastfeeding, you may feel a little like a dairy cow, endlessly getting your udders worked while you walk around topless more than you did on spring break. That's to be expected. As you adjust to the demands of breastfeeding, enlist people you trust to support you. Although you are doing the heavy lifting in the feeding department, breastfeeding shouldn't be solely a one-person job.

# IT WORKED FOR US

*Raffinee and Micaela, parents of a boy (2 years) and boy/girl twins (18 months)*

Born at 34 weeks, our babies had a short stay in the hospital while they learned how to eat. At first, I wasn't able to breastfeed and had to pump around the clock. Quite literally, I pumped every 1.5 hours during the day and twice during the night. Pumping was so much work, but it kept my milk supply up while the babies learned to latch. I had a hospital-grade breast pump, which was vital! At around two months old, one of my twins finally learned to latch. The other did it at three months old.

Sometimes I would do tandem feedings, but I found they could be overwhelming. The twins often distracted each other and didn't eat as well. Feeding them individually, although it was more work, allowed me to focus on helping them and bonding with them as individuals. I would assign each twin to a breast each day, to ensure equal feeding and emptying. For example, on Monday twin A would nurse on my left breast while twin B would nurse on my right. On Tuesday, twin A would get my right breast and twin B would get my left. After feeding, I would always pump to help further stimulate my breasts and to make sure I was empty. Again, it was a lot of work, but it allowed me to actually have a freezer stash of milk. I breastfed our twins for over a year and am incredibly proud of that accomplishment. For anyone hoping to do the same, I would definitely recommend renting a hospital-grade breast pump—it was worth its weight in gold! Or in this case, liquid gold! In addition, the Twin Z pillow was incredibly helpful. Even though I didn't tandem all that often, it was an invaluable resource when I did.

## NURSING NEEDS CHECKLIST

- ☐ Nursing bra

- ☐ Pump (we recommend a hands-free pump like the Willow)

- ☐ Pump parts (2 or 3 sets, including nipple shields)

  **Expert mom tip:** *Throw your dirty pump parts in a resealable plastic bag in the refrigerator. They can be safely stored for up to 24 hours before you need to wash them, which means you can use them for more pumpings before washing.*

- ☐ Kidney dishes from the hospital (Put one in your room so after a pumping in the middle of the night, you can soak the pump parts in water until you are ready to thoroughly clean in the morning.)

- ☐ Twin Z pillow or another nursing pillow

- ☐ Frozen nipple soothers

- ☐ Natural nipple cream (Motherlove is a great product.)

- ☐ Burp cloths

- ☐ Nursing tanks or tees

- ☐ Splurge: Buy a college-size mini fridge and keep by your bedside. This way you aren't running up and down the stairs in the middle of the night to store milk and pumping parts. If you have a mini fridge handy, you won't need to soak the pump parts in a kidney dish until morning (see Expert mom tip above).

# Breastfeeding Positions

Have you ever tried to juggle watermelons? Breastfeeding two babies at the same time—tandem feeding—might feel pretty similar. It will be awkward at first, but once you get the hang of it, it's not so tough. Learning to tandem feed will end up saving you a lot of time and will consequently get their schedules in sync, which is a *big win* for twin parents. Parenting really is a game of trial and error to ultimately find what works for your kids and your family. Breastfeeding your twins is no different. Luckily, there are several positions in which you can hold your babies to ensure a great latch and have a successful feeding experience for all.

DOUBLE FOOTBALL

Each baby's nursing needs are likely very different. One baby may struggle with latching while the other baby could hang off a cliff and still manage to get enough milk. If at first you don't succeed, don't give up. Try again, and don't hesitate to employ the help of an expert and your partner.

**Double football.** This is probably the most common tandem feeding position. The babies' feet slide under your armpits like little footballs, allowing their heads to rest facing your breasts.

**Front cross.** Holding both babies in a cradle position, cross their legs in front of one another, across your midline.

FRONT CROSS

UPRIGHT LATCH

**Upright latch.** This is a great position for babies with reflux. Your babies sit upright and nurse while you support their heads with your arms.

**Football and cradle.** This is similar to the football hold only both babies' bodies will be facing the same direction instead of tucking their legs underneath each of your arms.

Lactation consultants recommend that singleton parents begin each nursing session on a different side, either the left breast or right breast, which helps balance milk production in both breasts. Babies are the most efficient when they first begin nursing because they are hungry and more awake. As a nursing mom of twins, it is helpful to switch the side that each baby starts nursing on at each feeding, helping put equal demand on both breasts and maintaining your supply. It will help you *a lot* if you keep track of who was on each breast at the previous feed.

FOOTBALL AND CRADLE

jenn
says

After two weeks at home with our twins, my husband went back to work, which meant I had to master the tandem feed pretty quickly. This didn't only mean getting them to latch, feed, and burp at the same time, but I also had to get the babies to and from the nursing chair. I used the double My Brest Friend pillow as a tray. While the boys were lying in their crib, I would strap the pillow onto my waist, prop it up on the crib rail, and pick each baby up, one at a time, placing them on the pillow. Using my arms as a massive guardrail around them, I would support the underside of the pillow with my arms and their heads with my hands while I carried them the very short distance to the chair and back. This was a great solution until they were more wiggly, at which point I always had to be closer to the ground or on a flat, safe surface like my bed or the floor.

# Common Breastfeeding Issues

When it's 2 a.m. and you're alone in the dark with two babies, trying to ask the Google gods for answers to your breastfeeding woes, you'll be glad someone let you in one some breastfeeding 411 in advance. Here are five of the most common issues that may arise:

**Clogged ducts.** A clogged duct will feel like a hard pea in your breast because milk flow is obstructed. You may experience engorgement near the obstruction, tenderness, swelling, or redness. To help break up the clog, use vibration (like holding your electric toothbrush on the area), duct supplements (like WishGarden's Happy Ducts or lecithin), warm compresses, and massage.

**Blebs.** Blebs are calluses that form over nipple pores, a little like a pimple, and may be helped by soaking in Epsom salt baths and getting help from a lactation expert to correct your babies' latch.

**Trouble with or incorrect latches.** If it hurts, it's no good. Breastfeeding should not hurt. A bad latch can cause blebs or cracking, bleeding, and pain. Be sure to have the latch assessed by an expert and try an upright breastfeeding position.

**Sleepy baby.** Do you have a particularly sleepy baby who struggles to stay awake through an entire feeding? Solving this is as simple as providing constant stimulation. Try an upright breastfeeding position, unswaddling or undressing, or squirting a few drops of milk into your baby's mouth with a syringe to get them awake and nursing.

**Engorgement.** You will experience engorgement when your breasts are full and feeling painfully hard. With engorgement it is imperative that you keep the milk flowing. Pump more often to get milk out, use warm compresses, or a cold compress if you are dealing with an oversupply issue.

**Mastitis.** Mastitis is breast tissue inflammation and pain caused by an infection, but it isn't as common as people believe. The World

Health Organization states that it occurs in a variable percentage of lactating women, ranging from a few to 33 percent, but usually less than 10 percent. It normally occurs during the first six to 12 weeks of breastfeeding (most often in the first two to three weeks). Many women mistake symptoms of engorgement or clogged ducts for mastitis. Women with mastitis will experience flu-like symptoms and a fever of 101.3 degrees Fahrenheit or higher. If you experience any of these symptoms, nurse like crazy (it's absolutely safe to do so) and contact your doctor.

## IT WORKED FOR US!

*Amy, mother of Marley (7 years), Levi (5 years), and Micah and Hayden (3 years)*

When my twins were born I had a 2½ year-old son and 4-year-old daughter at home. After three weeks at home with my husband and my mom to help, I was a stay-at-home mom with four kids aged 4 and younger. I was on my own for most of the day. The process of feeding the twins and keeping my older children happy was a challenge. Between breastfeeding, burping, and changing the twins, the process could take an hour. My big kids were restless and wanting attention at that time, which made it even harder on everyone. I took my kids to Target and let the big kids each pick out one thing from the toy department. I told them it could be anything they wanted. This had never happened before and they were beyond excited. The caveat was they could only play with their new prizes when I was feeding the twins. So feeding the babies became an exciting time for the big kids because they could play with their new toys. As soon as feeding time was over, they had to put them away . . . until the next feeding.

# Feeding the Twins with Other Kids at Home

Before your twins arrive, establish routines for your other children that will help you keep them occupied while you are busy feeding the babies. We suggest creating several different "busy baskets" with a variety of independent, high-interest activities in them. Consider including the following:

+ Books appropriate for their age and reading level
+ Sticker books
+ Crayons, colored pencils, and washable markers
+ Magnetic toys—consider erasable drawing boards (Magna Doodles), blocks (Tegu wooden blocks), and tiles (Magna-Tiles)

Several times a day, set aside time when your little ones can be quietly engaged in these activities, and over a few weeks, gradually increase the time you expect them to occupy themselves. With any luck, by the time you bring the twins home, their siblings will mostly be able to settle into their busy box routines while you feed. Don't expect perfection here. Your kids will still need or want your attention and that is okay, but having at least some routine with expectations in place will help you feel more relaxed.

# Pumping

Although you can certainly feed your babies if you choose not to breastfeed, we like to tell breastfeeding mothers of twins to be prepared to pump at some point along the way. Pumping can be beneficial for a number of reasons. Having pumped breast milk on hand gives nursing mothers the freedom to allow others to help feed the babies. Also, breastfeeding is a feedback inhibitor loop, meaning that the more demand you place on your body to produce milk, the more it will produce. Pumping stimulates the breast without the baby, making your body believe it needs to produce more milk.

We found ourselves having a love-hate relationship with our breast pumps. The anticipation we felt while we waited to see how many ounces we would pump in one sitting, versus the dread we felt hooking that thing up to our chests, definitely plays with your mind at times. The truth is that pumping can feel like a chore. But before you write it off altogether, use these tips to make pumping manageable:

+ The minute you decide to pump, contact your insurance, as they are required to cover the cost and provide you with a pump. Save yourself some major dollar bills and take them up on it.

+ While in the hospital, you can borrow the hospital-grade pumps. You might even be able to pay a small rental fee and take it home.

+ Ask the lactation specialists in the hospital to properly fit you with correctly sized flanges (the funnels that look like they should be used in a science experiment). Each boob is differently shaped, which makes the fit of your flanges super important. Why? Because a good fit makes your nipples happy!

Remember this: happy nipples = happy breastfeeding. Lubricate your nipples with some olive oil or natural nipple cream to avoid chafing or cracks. Nobody wants chapped nipples. Not you, not your babies.

# Donor Milk

Donor milk comes from mothers who have been able to pump more milk than their babies can eat. It's a wonderful option when a mother cannot use her own milk, perhaps for one of the following reasons:

+ A mother's milk may be delayed or insufficiently established.

+ A mother may struggle to provide enough for multiple babies.

+ A mother may have a temporary breast infection that impacts production.

+ A mother may carry an infectious disease (HIV) or require medication that could pass through the breast milk.

+ A baby may be hospitalized and isn't able to be held or nursed.

You can absolutely use someone else's breast milk to feed your babies, but there are some things you should know. Donor milk from milk banks requires a prescription and is reserved for the most-at-risk infants, such as preterm or ill babies. The great news is that women who donate go through a stringent screening process, as does the donated milk. The milk will be tested for harmful bacteria and then pasteurized.

Some hospitals offer "compassionate milk," which can be given to moms who are struggling to adequately feed their babies but aren't high enough on the priority list to get milk from a bank. If "compassionate milk" isn't available, you can try to buy milk from a milk bank, but again, you will need a prescription. The cost of the milk (at the time of writing: approximatively $4.25/ounce) goes toward the cost of processing, handling, and distributing the milk. In some cases, donor milk may be covered by insurance, so be sure to check with your insurance company before you explore this option.

**jenn says**

After struggling with infertility, all I wanted was to control the decision about how I was going to feed my babies, which is why I set out to breastfeed, exclusively, for a year. But low supply issues soon made that a challenge. Luckily, my sister was nursing my nephew and was producing milk like a dairy cow. She was pumping to build a freezer stash and offered to donate some to us before she ultimately donated some to a milk bank. We first used donor milk in the hospital because both boys had lost more than 10 percent of their birth weight and my milk had not come in, so donor milk wasn't an unfamiliar idea to me when she offered to help. Her donation gave us a few more months exclusively with breast milk until I had to begin supplementing with formula.

# Milk Storage Guidelines

You know the saying, "There's no crying over spilled milk"? Well, that probably won't hit home until it happens to you. Breast milk and formula have specific guidelines for storage. Keeping these handy and following them closely is important for the safety of your babies.

## Breast Milk

Remember the rule of six. Freshly expressed breast milk can remain at room temperature for six hours, be refrigerated for six days, or kept in a refrigerator-style freezer for six months (12 months in a deep freezer). Once frozen it cannot be refrozen and must be consumed within 24 hours of thawing. Don't shake breast milk, warm it in a microwave, or add freshly expressed milk to thawed milk. In general, microwaving food can have a negative impact on the nutrients. This can be translated to breast milk as well, although there isn't much evidence out there to support that. More important, microwaving and stove-top heating causes "hot spots" in the milk, which can burn your baby.

Shaking breast milk isn't recommended because it could break down the proteins in the milk. However, you would have to shake rather vigorously. Experts suggest that you swirl the milk until the cream is combined into the milk.

Some experts suggest that adding freshly expressed milk to older milk is done only after the freshly expressed milk has been refrigerated long enough to be the same temperature. There really isn't a scientific reason why you cannot mix two batches of milk together when they have been expressed a few days apart.

**meghan says**

I had finally gotten to a point where pumping was going pretty well, milk was flowing, and my boobs and I couldn't be happier. After the most epic pumping session ever, I set the pump down, tried to unhook my pumping bra, and *bam!* Milk flew everywhere. My husband came running to see if I was okay and there I was—topless, holding an empty bottle, and tears running down my face. I know this sounds silly, but that stuff is like gold! Nobody wants to spill an ounce of that stuff. If it happens, you absolutely have a pass to be upset.

## TWINCREDIBLE

*Sarah, mother of four children, including twin boys (5 years)*

Nursing twins is probably one of my fondest memories. It wasn't easy at first, but when you start to get the hang of tandem nursing two babies, it is magic. I remember many occasions when they would be happily nursing away and would reach for each other to hold hands (and your heart melts and milk explodes). Those are the moments that make you believe you can keep going with twins even when it's hard. The love and bond that twins share is deep and powerful, and getting to be a part of it has been my joy and honor.

### Formula

Twin parents using formula often make large batches to avoid making bottles every feeding. Formula can be made and kept in the refrigerator for 24 hours. Ready-made formula—not the powder kind—can be kept in a refrigerator for 48 hours. Once a baby has taken some formula from a bottle, any remaining formula in the bottle must be consumed within one hour or be thrown away.

## Building Supply

Ask any breastfeeding mother what she Googled today and she may very well tell you she was trying to find a way to build up her milk supply. Nursing two babies isn't the easiest task, and the worry moms feel about whether their babies are getting enough food can be overwhelming. Challenges you may face with low supply aren't related to things you are doing right or wrong per se, but they do have a lot to do with underlying hormonal or anatomical issues. If your babies are gaining weight appropriately then it's probably safe to assume that you don't have a supply issue. It's not uncommon for mothers to gauge their supply or lack thereof by the amount of milk they pump. There are a number of things you can do to help maintain a healthy supply and successfully feed your babies. And if you run into roadblocks, give it your best shot and be forgiving of yourself, because feeding two babies is demanding.

Keep these tips in mind to keep your supply flowing:

**Hydrate, and hydrate some more.** We cannot emphasize this enough. Drinking a lot of water throughout the day is extremely important for nursing mothers. We both lugged around those amazing water bottles from the hospital without shame.

**Don't forget to eat.** This sounds so simple, yet when you are feeding, burping, and changing babies around the clock, it can be easy to put your most basic needs on the back burner. It is important to listen to your body and eat whenever you feel hungry. Now is not the time for a calorie-restricted diet.

Since your average calorie intake will be slightly higher while you are nursing, it is fun to indulge every now and again, but try to focus the majority of your calorie intake on healthy, milk-friendly foods such as apricots, blueberries, oatmeal, oranges, spinach, and seeds (like sesame, poppy, caraway, anise, and coriander).

**Prioritize the pump.** Adding one or two pumping sessions into your day helps empty your breasts more often, signaling to your body that it needs to produce more milk.

**Consider adding supplements into your diet.** Fenugreek, blessed thistle, and alfalfa have been shown to increase milk production. Just remember that these are most effective when combined with frequent breastfeeding or pumping.

jenn says

Jenn says: I took a breastfeeding class specifically for parents who are expecting twins. When my husband and I sat down in our class, the first thing we heard was the instructor say, "Anyone can breastfeed and make enough milk to feed any number of babies." I thought, well, okay then, anyone can do this and that will be exactly how this goes. I didn't understand enough about breastfeeding to know that it's not true, and I fought for eight months under the illusion that my challenges were because I had done something wrong. For a long time, I believed that I ruined my supply because I went to a football game and skipped one pumping session because I refused to sit and pump in that stadium restroom one more time. There were probably underlying causes of our challenges, but if I had been more educated about the whole thing, I might not have been so unnecessarily hard on myself.

# TIPS FROM A PRO: BREASTFEEDING TROUBLESHOOTING

*Margaret Emmerich, IBCLC, CLC, CLE*

Carrying and delivering two babies is hard work, not just for mama, but for the babies as well. Space limitations often lead to some very creative twin positioning in utero, or the method of delivery can have an impact on a baby post-birth. Once they've arrived, you might find that one of your milk monsters is having a hard time latching, bobs on and off the breast, or seems disorganized. If so, the culprit may be a kink in tight neck muscles. Torticollis is the name for this neck stiffness. Your baby may need a relaxing massage to work the kinks out, loosen tight muscles, and get all the nerves firing properly. Seek the help of an International Board Certified Lactation Consultant (IBCLC) who will be able to refer you to different bodyworkers such as chiropractors, cranial sacral therapists, or osteopaths. Their services are likely to be covered by insurance, but it's always good to check. Once you get your baby's neck moving properly, you'll be back on the path to blissful breastfeeding!

## Introducing a Bottle

Repeat after us: Bottle feeding doesn't ruin breastfeeding. That's right. Repeat that over and over. After breastfeeding has been well established (generally after one month to six weeks), feel free to begin introducing a bottle during one or two feedings a day. Keep these tips in mind:

+ **Use slow-flow nipples.** This makes getting milk from a bottle equally as challenging as getting milk from the breast. You can test your slow-flow nipple by turning the bottle upside down; the milk should not drip out.

+ **Slowly introduce larger nipples as your babies develop.** One sign your babies might be ready for a larger nipple size is when they start to

## Alcohol and Breastfeeding

Maybe you had an aversion to alcohol while you were pregnant and just the smell made you run for the toilet, but now a glass of wine or a cocktail sounds delightful. As two wine-loving mamas, we thought it appropriate to touch upon how to indulge in an adult beverage while you are breastfeeding.

The Centers for Disease Control and Prevention suggests that moderate alcohol consumption, defined as one drink per day, likely will not harm your babies. Since alcohol can be passed on to your babies through breast milk, it is suggested that mothers wait two hours after enjoying *one* drink before nursing again.

You don't have to turn down the invitation for a night out simply because you are breastfeeding. Yes, pumping and dumping feels a little like a form of self-sabotage, but it doesn't have to be your only solution. You can also plan your drinks according to the two-hour rule as well.

cry during bottle feeding—this could be an indicator that they're frustrated by the slow flow.

+ **Feed your babies in an upright position.** Help them by holding the bottle in a horizontal position (without forcing the nipple into their mouths), and keeping the nipple of the bottle half full, which allows you to help control the milk flow.

Introducing a bottle not only gives nursing moms a little more freedom and flexibility but also allows your partner to be part of the process and bond with the babies. It can also ease the transition if you are preparing to go back to work. Your partner clearly won't experience the intimacy of breastfeeding, but they can absolutely experience a beautiful bond with their babies by participating in feedings. Whether you decide to pump breast milk or use formula, bottle feeding can be a great way for partners to develop that special connection with their children.

Women birth the babies and will naturally have a special bond with them, but it is important to consider all members of the family and allow them to be part of this special process. In a two-mom parenting team, the woman who gave birth may naturally take on a motherly role. It doesn't mean that the other mother doesn't have a maternal role; however, it could be easy to feel sideswiped of that initial bonding. In a two-dad partnership, neither parents birthed the babies. Dads, get as much skin-to-skin time with each of your babies as possible, from birth, and continue to deepen your connection with your babies by sharing the feeding responsibilities.

meghan
says

My husband and I took shifts during the night when he went back to work at around four weeks after birth. We would use the Twin Z pillow, plop the pillow on the floor, and feed in the nursery. Not only was this convenient, but it was a cozy environment in the quiet nursery that didn't disrupt their sleep. It was nice that my husband could take both boys for the 11 p.m. feeding while I slept a longer leg. Then I tagged in for the 2 a.m. feeding while he got rested up for work.

## For the Working Mom

Sleep deprivation and trying to juggle feeding and sleeping schedules require a person to work a little magic on a daily basis. Going back to work, coupled with your plan to continue breastfeeding your babies, can result in feeling anxious and uneasy about the whole thing. Pumping at home is a big task, but pumping at work presents a whole new set of challenges. Doing a little homework before your maternity leave ends will help ease your stresses and make your transition back to work a little more seamless, even though there may still be tears shed.

- Work on your production ahead of time by adding one or two extra pumping sessions to your routine. Instead of using the milk immediately, stash it in the freezer to build up your stock.

- As a breastfeeding mother at work, your employer is required by law to provide you with a private place to pump that is not a bathroom. You also must be allowed a reasonable amount of "break" time to pump at work (for up to one year) after your babies are born.

- As you feel comfortable, discuss your anticipated pumping schedule with your employer to ensure that everyone understands your intentions.

- Take advantage of your benefits by allowing your insurance to provide you with a pump, and invest in a second pump and spare parts to be kept at work. We were recently introduced to the Willow, a wearable breast pump that can be worn in your bra, under your clothes, without cords or bottles attached. That gadget is a game-changer for every breastfeeding mother!

- Be sure that you have proper storage for your pumped milk.

- Consider on-demand feedings on the weekends to help boost your supply and spend a little more time bonding with your babies.

## Breastfeeding FAQ

After navigating our own breastfeeding journeys and supporting many other twin moms as they find their groove, we have put together a list of the most common questions or concerns we have come across to help put your mind at ease as you prepare to feed your own babies.

## How long will it take to breastfeed both babies?

Typically, newborns take about 20 to 45 minutes to breastfeed, which should speed up as your baby becomes more awake and learns to efficiently nurse.

## One baby is a champion breastfeeder, the other not so much. What should I do?

First and foremost, get help from a certified lactation expert to troubleshoot your challenging eater. The more support you can gather, the more successful your breastfeeding experience will be. Before tossing in the towel altogether, try some of these other options, too.

+ Consider feeding one baby via breast and the other with a pumped bottle.

+ Try feeding one baby at a time, the struggling baby first, to see if you can master their latch, or if they will perform better without distractions.

## I'm stressed to the max when it comes to breastfeeding. Should I quit?

We get it. Your dream was to breastfeed. It was our dream, too. But if, after trying all the nursing tricks—everything from lactation cookies to special vitamins—you haven't been able to find your groove, give yourself permission to *let it go*.

The truth is that in the end, being fed is what is best.

## My babies hate taking a bottle and insist on my breasts. I'm exhausted. What can I do?

Feeling like a milk machine is exhausting, which is why people elect to introduce bottles to their babies. With that, however, can come the problem of bottle refusal, turning mama's new sidekicks into permanent attachments. Consult your lactation expert and try the following:

+ Choose a breast-like bottle.

+ Time your introduction so that your babies aren't hungry, tired, or distracted so they remember the bottle as a positive experience.

+ Often, the non-nursing partner can be more successful at introducing bottles because babies can smell the boob from miles away.

+ Feed in any position but avoid a cradle position when bottle feeding.

## I am still nursing my 18-month old. Can I continue to nurse her once my twins are born?

Absolutely. The thing to know is that your milk content will change to meet the needs of your growing infants, which could mean that your older child may not love the taste of your breast milk when that happens. About halfway through your pregnancy, your milk will turn to colostrum, which has a higher sodium content, making your milk taste saltier. It isn't unusual for an older child to naturally wean themselves at that point. If this doesn't happen and they continue to nurse once the twins are born, nurse the twins first and then give the other their turn.

# Formula Feeding

Let's get real. Breastfeeding is not always easy, and here you are, trying to feed two at one time. Think for a minute: What does being a parent really mean? It is a whole lot more than feeding your baby. Maybe breastfeeding isn't for you—that's okay! Do you feel the weight of social pressure about your choice to formula feed? Kick the shamers to the curb and walk around confidently knowing that you are making a perfectly valid choice as a responsible parent.

# Supplementing Breast Milk with Formula

Supplementing is often suggested to parents when breast-feeding challenges arise. Following our belief that fed is best, we absolutely endorse supplementing with formula, your own pumped breast milk, or even donor milk. What you should know is that supplementing doesn't have to mean the end of breastfeeding. There are ways to manage supplementing while still meeting your breastfeeding goals. If supplementation is suggested to you, keep these things in mind:

+ Pump regularly to help increase your milk supply.
+ Supplement at the breast, while your child is nursing. You can use syringes or even a tube that slides into a baby's mouth, helping your child associate the breast with food.
+ If supplementing with a bottle, give the bottle first and finish the feeding with the breast. This will help your infants associate a feeling of satisfaction with breastfeeding rather than the bottle.

## Choosing a Formula

The formula market today has come a long way, which means that parents are faced with a million formula choices. While the brand doesn't necessarily matter (the FDA regulates the nutritional requirements so formula contains all the nutrients your babies need) there are different types of formula to choose from. Knowing what your options are and how they may benefit your babies will help you narrow down your choices. The American Academy of Pediatrics does recommend that you choose an iron-fortified formula.

A lot of babies do well with cow's milk formulas, and the need to use a different type of formula varies greatly from child to child.

Before jumping to a hydrolyzed (which contains partially broken-down proteins that can be easier to digest), soy-based, lactose-free, or hypoallergenic type, consult your doctor and be sure to give your baby enough time with one formula before you switch to another. If you introduce formula to your babies in the hospital, and the hospital brand works for them, snag as much as you can to use at home.

Each type of formula will usually come in a powder form (least expensive, easy to travel with, more prep time), a concentrate (add water, but a little pricier) or a ready-made form (least amount of prep time, but the most expensive).

## Gear and Gadgets

As a formula-feeding parent, you will naturally have more gear to manage, but not all of it is a must-have. This table will help you get started with the things you definitely will need, and suggest the other things that might make life a little less complicated.

## Formula Feeding Checklist

### MUST-HAVES

- [ ] Bottles
- [ ] Nipples (variety of flow levels)
- [ ] Dr. Brown's formula pitcher
- [ ] Kidney dish from the hospital (keep one upstairs so that after a night feeding you can soak dirty bottles in water and then wash in the morning)
- [ ] Bottle brush
- [ ] Bottle drying rack (we *love* the Boon GRASS)
- [ ] Burp cloths
- [ ] Medela microwave sanitizing bags (quick and easy way to disinfect)
- [ ] Nursing pillows (such as Boppys) or Twin Z pillow to lay babies in while bottle feeding

### CAN BE HELPFUL TO HAVE

- [ ] Formula dispenser
- [ ] Bottle warmer
- [ ] Bottle maker like the Baby Brezza

meghan
says

Dr. Brown's makes an awesome formula pitcher. I made a pitcher of formula daily to save time. I was able to prep all the bottles we needed for the day, leaving me with less to do later! The best bottles out there for formula-feeding parents who are often on the go are Mixie bottles. I discovered these and went a bit overboard, buying an entire case! I used about six total and gave the rest away as gifts. Mixie bottles are convenient because they allow you to store pre-measured formula in the bottom of the bottle, while the water is contained in a separate compartment. When you are out and about, simply pop the button on the bottom of the Mixie bottle, releasing the formula into the water, shake, and boom! Feeding on the go made simple.

## Bottles and Nipples

Bottles and nipples and bottles, oh my! The choice of bottles and types of nipples is overwhelmingly large. Nowadays you can choose from a variety of brands, shapes, and materials. Bottles are usually made of glass, plastic, silicone, or even stainless steel, while nipples are silicone and sometimes latex.

The thing to know about choosing a nipple is that the shape and flow rate will make a difference. There are dome-shaped nipples and flat nipples that more closely mimic a real nipple. And then there is the flow rate, which refers to the size of the hole in the top of the nipple. A Level 1 nipple is suitable for newborns, moving up in level from there.

Before you head out and buy a million different bottles and nipples, either buy a single bottle from a few different brands or collect hand-me-downs from friends and invest in new nipples. It is impossible to predict which bottle and nipple either of your babes will like before they get to experience a few different options. Save your money and cabinet space until your babies declare their preferences and then go shopping.

## IT WORKED FOR US

*Vanessa, mother of Miles and Oliver (6 years)*

The reality for any twin parent—and particularly a single parent—is that you aren't always going to have two sets of hands around at feeding time. Best MacGyver moment: using stuffed animals to prop bottles on so the babies could drink on their own. In the beginning I would start Miles first (my faster drinker) and then Oliver a minute or two later so I could burp them each about halfway through. Eventually, I was able to use this time and system to trim finger and toe nails while the boys were still and calm. Once they could hold their own bottles and no longer needed burping, I would sit between them with a cup of tea, talk to them, and enjoy!

# Formula Feeding FAQ

Between the two of us, we had four babies all being formula fed at some point, which means we had our own sets of worries and uncertainties. Here you will find the most commonly asked questions from parents who have decided to go with formula.

## Do I need to warm up formula before feeding it to my babies?

The decision whether to warm up formula is 100 percent up to the parents, but it's not necessary at all. Babies can and will take a bottle that is warm, room temperature, or even chilled. Much of the advice we give people about sleep issues with infants is all about what you are willing to do as a parent, long term. The same thing applies to feeding your baby. If you are willing to find a way to warm a bottle at 2 a.m., when you're still half asleep, then by all means warm up that bottle. If not, try feeding your baby room-temperature formula or even a bottle straight from the refrigerator.

**Expert mom tip:** *If you want to warm bottles or it seems to be your babies' preference, don't spend money on a bottle warmer. Simply run your Keurig without the coffee and use the hot water to warm your bottles. It usually only takes two or three minutes. Don't have a Keurig? Piping hot water from the tap will accomplish the same thing.*

## I feel guilty for not breastfeeding. How can I get over this feeling and move on, and quit comparing myself to my breastfeeding friends?

We live in a "breast is best" world. Thanks to the Internet and social media, it's easy to compare our circumstances with others and get caught up in a cycle of guilt. Stop that *now*! You are doing the best that you possibly can for your babies, so you do you!

If you gave it your best shot and it didn't work out, that's okay. If you didn't want to breastfeed at all, that's okay, too. There is no room for judgment here. Know that you are doing an amazing job as a parent and that formula babies still grow up to be well-adjusted humans. No one will be standing around at a college party talking about how they were fed as infants, anyway, so try not to get caught up in the comparison game because all that does is make you feel bad.

## Formula feeding is expensive. How can I cut down on the cost?

The cost of formula for two babies can add up quickly, but don't fret: There are some savvy strategies to minimize the impact it has on your pocketbook. Here are five ways parents can save:

1. Stick with powder; it is the least expensive option.

2. Ask for samples at the doctor's office. Pediatricians often get boxes of samples that they are more than happy to hand out. All you have to do is ask.

3. If your babies will tolerate them, stick to generic brands.

4. Buy formula in bulk at stores like Costco or Sam's Club.

5. Visit the websites of formula companies and join their mailing lists or membership clubs. Just for joining they will send you coupons for free or discounted formula. Make sure your partner signs up for the mailing lists as well . . . who doesn't want to double the discounts?

## My baby or babies are super fussy. Should I switch their formula?

Fussy babies are fairly normal, and their fussiness can be attributed to a variety of reasons. Sometimes a simple burp will ease their tummies and they are good to go. If your baby is arching their back, that may be sign of reflux. If they are curling in a ball, that is a sign of gas. Allergies will come with symptoms like vomiting, diarrhea, or blood in their stools. As always, the best bet is to consult the pediatrician before you make any drastic changes to your babies' diet. A doctor will be able to confirm that a change in formula is necessary and guide you on how to switch things up without disrupting their digestion.

# Nighttime Feedings

All new parents will have some questions about feeding babies during the night. Most of this information is tucked here and there in this book, but we thought it would help to gather some answers in one place so you can feel a bit more confident about what to expect.

Typically, newborn babies will feed on demand (when they indicate that they are hungry), usually every 1 to 3 hours, or 8 to 12 times in 24 hours. These feedings will take anywhere from 20 to 45 minutes, but this will improve as your baby is more awake and becomes more efficient at nursing. You should know that there isn't a specified amount of time a baby should feed, so let your babies indicate that the feeding is over when they stop sucking for longer than a minute or two. Formula-fed babies will typically take 2 to 4 ounces every two to four hours.

You might have heard the term *dream feed*. A dream feed is a feeding that parents initiate by rousing their sleeping babies just enough to nurse or bottle feed them in a very drowsy state. The timing is usually when the parents are going to bed—between 10 p.m. and 12 a.m. Many parents choose to feed the babies right before their own bedtime, setting themselves up for as long a sleep stretch as possible given the babies full bellies. There are different opinions on how well this works and even whether it's smart to wake your sleeping babies. We suggest talking to friends with children to hear about their experiences with dream feeds, to help you determine if you might want to try them.

Extra help for parents of twins is an invaluable resource and something you should accept willingly. When family and friends offer to jump in, take them up on it without hesitation. If your finances allow, consider hiring a night nurse or night nanny, as it may just be some of the best money you ever spent. Contrary to popular belief, you aren't just paying for a good night's sleep. In fact, you are making an investment in your parenting by hiring a professional who has extensive training not only in newborn care (specifically in breast and bottle feeding, as well as sleep training), but also in the postpartum care of mothers.

## Tips for Nighttime Feedings

Here are our top recommendations for making nighttime feedings in the first few weeks more efficient:

+ Get professional help from the beginning, before leaving the hospital. Whether you are breastfeeding or bottle feeding, the lactation consultants and nurses can help you troubleshoot and ensure things are going well from the get-go, meaning you can leave the hospital feeling confident.

+ Use extra hands whenever and as often as available.

- Set up a feeding station (or a few around the house) stocked with supplies and necessities. Always feed in one of those stations. The more routine you are, the more efficient you will be.

- Feed your babies at the same time when you are comfortable.

- Adapt when things are not working for you or your babies. Use a different pillow, try a different position, move locations, etc.

*Breastfeeding-specific tips:*
- Make sure (with the help of an IBCLC) that your babies are latching properly. Then practice a lot so that latching becomes second nature to them.

- Once your babies are latching well, work to perfect your tandem feeding with the support of the lactation professionals in the hospital. While the choice to tandem feed is personal, feeding your babies at the same time does save time.

- Try different positions until you find one that works.

- Get a hospital-grade pump and use it to increase your supply if needed.

*Formula/bottle feeding-specific tips:*
- Make formula in large batches (enough for 24 hours) and store in the refrigerator.

- Get everything ready, including bottles poured and warmed (if you choose), before sitting down.

- Invest in a Twin Z nursing pillow. It is a great tool for bottle-feeding parents to lay babies together and feed simultaneously.

- Use slow-flow nipples.

jenn says

A few weeks after our twins were born, a dear family friend, who happens to be a NICU nurse, offered to come over for a night to allow us to get a good night's sleep.

While it was difficult to ask a friend to stay up all night with our babies, it was the best gift we were offered. After that one night, we felt refreshed and reenergized and realized that we needed a little more nighttime help. Knowing this, we began to explore the option of a night nanny. The woman we hired was so much more than a night nurse. Ultimately, she taught me everything I needed to know about babies, helped troubleshoot when challenges arose, and was an unwavering support while I adjusted to motherhood. Her support and knowledge were invaluable for an overwhelmed new mom. In choosing to hire her I became a confident mom and gained a friend.

## IT WORKED FOR US

*Meghan, mother of Olive and Willow (4 years) and Piper (2 years)*

I was always hoping I'd be able to tandem breastfeed my twins. I didn't know if it would be possible but I wanted to try! They were born a month premature and Olive ended up in the NICU. She was too small and weak to breastfeed so she was fed by syringe or bottle, receiving formula until my milk came in. As a result, I learned how to breastfeed with Willow until Olive was strong enough. At five weeks they were both nursing and I decided to try tandem! I used the My Brest Friend nursing pillow, which was amazing. It meant I was fully supported and got them in a good position to nurse. My go-to nursing position was the football hold. I nursed them tandem until they were about nine months! I used the time when I was nursing to watch shows on my iPad and always had lots of snacks and water nearby. It's amazing how thirsty and hungry you get while feeding two babies! Just don't forget to have everything nearby before you are locked down in your nursing position, because once you're settled, there is no getting up for a while!

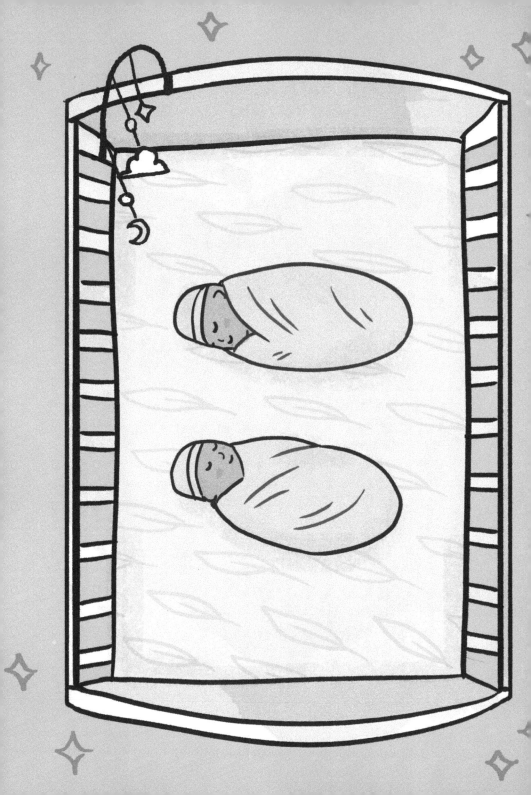

# Sleeping

A few weeks after the babies are born, there is a good chance you'll be powering through on very little sleep. It's perfectly normal, and it's worth pointing out that the extreme sleep deprivation of the early weeks is temporary. In this chapter, we share the facts of infant sleep so that you know what to expect and how to teach healthy sleep habits to your children. Interrupted and fragmented sleep is not only hard on you, the parents, but is challenging for your babies as well. When everyone is well rested we are all healthier, happier, better-functioning people. This chapter will help you set realistic expectations and teach you some simple strategies to make quality sleep achievable.

# Baby Sleep in Brief

Whether you are a first-time parent or you have done this before, infant sleep can be a tricky beast to tackle. It may sound crazy because it seems like sleep should be automatic, but babies don't naturally know how to fall asleep or stay asleep on their own. It is our job as parents to teach them, which means that arming yourself with an understanding of how sleep develops in babies is a necessity. It might not be a fix-all for the exhaustion we inevitably experience as new parents, but having this knowledge will help you tackle sleep issues more successfully.

The reality of actual sleep time versus awake time for newborns is pretty astounding. Did you know that in the first few weeks of life your newborns will probably sleep for about 16 hours of a 24-hour day? That's a lot of snoozing. It doesn't leave many hours that your babies are awake and, when they are, chances are they are eating.

## Infant Sleep Cycles

A sleep cycle for an average adult is 70 to 100 minutes. For infants, it is much shorter, typically ranging from 45 to 60 minutes. Fifty percent of a baby's sleep is spent in light, active (REM) sleep, which is what causes babies to wake more easily. Because baby sleep is mostly REM or light sleep, they can struggle to transition from sleep cycle to sleep cycle.

The single biggest frustration we hear about is night wakings—those times in the night when parents (who would otherwise be peacefully sleeping) must get their babies back to sleep because they haven't yet learned to fall asleep independently. Swaddles and white noise are great tools for helping your babies stay asleep and transition between sleep cycles smoothly, as is working to teach your babies the skill of self-soothing early on.

## Startle Reflex

Babies are born with a variety of reflexes, the most common being the startle, or Moro, reflex. Loud noises or the feeling that they are falling may cause your babies to startle, which is why they throw their arms and legs outward. This plays a role in sleep because the startle reflex can wake a sleeping baby, undoing all the hard work you put into getting them to sleep. Luckily, this reflex usually disappears between three and six months. Again, being tightly swaddled and in a room filled with white noise can help babies stay asleep or go back to sleep if the reflex startles them awake.

## Sleep Cues

It seems counterintuitive, but overtired babies have more difficulty falling asleep and staying asleep. Overtiredness induces a stress-response system, causing the body to produce more cortisol and adrenaline to stay awake. Watching for early tiredness cues helps prevent an unwanted outcome—inconsolable, overtired babies who uncomfortably arch their backs and resist your efforts to put them to sleep, even through nursing or bottle feeding. It would seem natural that "wearing a baby out" would help them sleep better and longer, but that is not the case at all.

If you only remember one thing about infant sleep, remember that *sleep begets sleep*. In other words, well-rested babies will typically be better sleepers, waking you up less often. One key to helping your twins get to sleep easily is being able to recognize their sleep cues. Here are some cues to look out for:

+ Rubbing their eyes, hair, or ears

+ Yawning

+ Starting to look grumpy

As infants age and are able to focus more and for longer periods of time, additional indicators that they are growing tired include avoiding eye contact with you and losing interest in their favorite toys.

Once you recognize these signs, there are several tools you can use to set the stage for sleep:

+ Move into a quiet room and turn on white noise

+ Dim the lights

+ Swaddle your babies

+ Rock them to get them sleepy (but not asleep)

+ Feed them (again, until sleepy but not asleep)

If one or both of your babies is perpetually overtired, you may begin to see them:

+ Sleeping less than the recommended average for their age

+ Fighting daytime feedings but feeding well at night

+ Displaying extreme fussiness, especially as the day goes on

+ Showing signs of separation anxiety and only wanting to be held and rocked

With a little practice, you can begin to read the signs of your babies' tiredness, helping them get the sleep that they need and leaving you frustration-free.

# IT WORKED FOR US

*Paige, mother of Elise and Miles (4 months) and Brice (3 years)*

One day, my 4-week-old twins had been awake for almost three consecutive hours, and my 2-year-old was way past his nap time. Do you know what three overtired children in the same house sound like? It made me want to hide in the pantry with a pint of ice cream. But instead I did a quick YouTube search and found a tutorial for how to carry both twins in a sling. I put on the Boba wrap, nestled them in, and started bouncing them to sleep while my 2-year-old serenaded me with "Old MacDonald." Once the babies calmed down, I got my toddler up to his room and had him pretend to be a monkey so I could hoist him into his crib with my free arm. Closing the door behind me and looking at the twins sleeping peacefully in the wrap, it was one of those "I've totally got this!" moments. And that wrap continues to save us whenever I've got an overtired baby (or babies) on my hands.

## Day versus Night Confusion

Why does it always seem like you can never get a grip on your jet lag after returning home from a relaxing trip? Well, it's actually pretty similar to the issue that parents have when their babies get daytime confused with nighttime. We all have something called a circadian rhythm, which refers to our "internal clock," that signals to our body when it is time to sleep and time to be awake in 24-hour intervals. Babies' "internal clocks" usually begin to develop in the first two to four months.

Think back to pregnancy. Do you remember how active your babies seemed at night? They acted as if they were at a nightclub while you were trying to get some shut eye at 8:00 p.m. Movement during the day lulled your babies to sleep, but as soon as you stopped moving around so much (because you yourself were sleeping), your babies were *wide awake* and *wiggly*! In the womb, your babies relied on you and your hormones to help them sleep, but once they are born, they must rely on their own internal clocks, which at birth aren't yet developed.

Therefore, parents often find that newborns sleep more during the day, which means they can be more awake and active at night. You can help your babies develop their circadian rhythm in a few ways:

+ Bring more natural light and activity into your home during the day.

+ Talk and interact with them as much as possible during their wakeful hours.

+ As bedtime approaches, begin signaling that it is time to sleep with dimmed lights and less noise.

+ When interacting with your babies during the night for feedings and diaper changes, keep it minimal, being sure that the activity is as quiet and stimulation free.

## Routine, Routine, Routine

Babies thrive on routine. Whether you are overly organized or as laid back as they come, instilling a solid bedtime routine for your babies will help you establish solid sleep habits. After you establish a sleep routine they will always know one thing: Sleep is coming. Whether they are ready to go to bed is another story, but letting them know sleep is coming at least helps move things along.

In the early weeks, scheduling is out of the question with newborn babies. However, in as early as six to eight weeks, you can begin to establish a bedtime routine to help you reinforce healthy sleep habits. While you won't necessarily have your babies on a predicable sleep schedule until closer to 12 weeks, when sleep patterns become more regular, setting up routines early lays a solid foundation for the work that you will do later.

How in the world do you establish a bedtime routine? Set the mood. Have you ever lit a few candles, poured a glass of wine, and thrown on some music to set the mood with your partner? Approach it more or less the same with your babies, minus the romance. Establish a few steps that you do in a similar order every night during bedtime. There isn't a perfect equation for bedtime routines, and it can change as babies get older. If you have a late night or get back from soccer practice with another kid just in time for bed, still go through an abbreviated version of your routine to help prepare your babies for sleep.

From start to finish, our bedtime routine should be no longer than 30 minutes and can be as short as 10 minutes for very young babies. Whatever you decide to include, stick to the *same order* every single night. Here are a few of our favorite bedtime rituals that you might want to incorporate into your routine:

**Dim lights.** Set the mood and create a space that says it's time to sleep. Turn down the lights as the very first step.

**Bath.** You don't need to bathe a baby every single day. Even a simple wipe down will do.

**Diaper change.** After a bath or wipe down, change diapers so they're fresh. No one wants to go to bed wet! And yes, of course your babies will wet their diapers as soon as you change them. That is one of nature's little jokes you'll laugh at on some days and cry at on others.

**Massage.** Lather on some baby lotion and gently massage your babies. Many parents look for fragrance-free lotion to make sure nothing irritates their babies' skin. It's extremely soothing and a great way to calm them before bed.

**Rocking chair.** Rocking your babies in your arms while feeding, singing, or reading is a nice way to bond at the end of each day.

**Books.** Even brand-new babies will listen to you read them books. Not only does it help develop early literacy skills (yes, even this early, according to an article in *Reading Rockets*), but it will help them fall asleep, too.

**Lullaby.** Warm up those pipes. Babies love to hear a sweet song and the voices of their parents are calming, even if you didn't make the Billboard Hot 100. Sing something you love or make it up, but sing, as it helps calm babies into a sleepy state.

**Bottle or breast.** Feed your babies before bedtime as part of your routine. Make sure this is the last step before laying them in their cribs, so their bellies are full as they are ready to snooze.

**Independent sleep.** As early as possible (but typically after about six weeks), begin teaching your babies to fall asleep independently. Lay them down in a very drowsy state, but with their eyes still open slightly. We know what you're thinking. Your newborns fall asleep at every feeding, so laying them down awake is downright impossible! But it is possible. As their sleep matures and they grow out of that newborn sleepiness, wake them just enough to see the whites of their eyes before laying them down. The ability to fall asleep independently is a vital component to training your babies to sleep, and it can be more challenging to teach as babies get used to any "props." On that note, turn to page 124 for a quick introduction to sleep associations.

**White noise.** Using a white noise machine can mimic sounds similar to that of your womb, which is comforting to your babies. White noise also helps babies sleep through a lot of noise (like each other) they otherwise wouldn't tune out. Some people like to leave the white noise machine as one of the last steps to their routine, after books are read, lullabies are sung, and it is really time to hit the sack.

Certainly, you don't need to find a way to make time for all of this every single night; after all, there are bottles to wash and, if you manage to make the time, glasses of wine to consume. Do, however, pick a few that work for your family and stick to them. A consistent bedtime routine established within the first few months of life sets everyone up for success by preparing for what's to come: sleep.

meghan says

Some of the best advice we received was to establish a bedtime routine with our boys around six weeks old. While sleep was still somewhat unpredictable at this age, we were reassured that this would be a fundamental step in getting our boys to sleep like champs. To this day, if we need to modify our bedtime routine because we have been at a backyard barbecue and just didn't get home on time, we stay the course. Granted, we can accomplish our routine in five minutes now if need be, but we still dim the lights, wipe the boys down with baby wipes or a damp cloth (who needs a bath after the pool anyway?), turn on the white noise, and say our prayers. Simple, easy, and most important, it's all done with consistency so they know that sleep is coming.

## The Value of Scheduling Sleep

To schedule sleep is to establish set times when you will put your babies down for naps and for sleep at night. This is different from sleep training, which is a structured approach to helping your babies sleep through the night and learning how to fall back asleep independently if they wake. In this chapter we focus mostly on sleep scheduling, starting with young infants. We briefly address sleep training later on, which doctors typically do not recommend undertaking before your babies are about 12 weeks of age or have at least doubled their birthweight.

Some parents decide that their babies' lives (as well as their own) revolve around sleep and will always get them home to sleep in their cribs for bedtime and nap time. Others prefer a more on-the-go lifestyle and expect their babies to sleep in car seats and at their siblings' sporting events. We will say this: When it comes to sleep, find what works for you and stick to it! We strongly believe that there is serious value in keeping your twins on a schedule because it brings predictability when everything else can feel chaotic. That motivated us, and scheduling worked for us. If you think sleep scheduling might work for you, too, our advice is to start scheduling sleep when the babies are between 6 and 8 weeks old. Essential preparation for scheduling includes tracking the babies' sleep patterns, laying them down at the same time, staying away from negative sleep associations, and using consistent routines to indicate that sleep is coming.

# Sleep Associations

What do you do each night before you crawl into bed? Personally, we like to slip into comfy pajamas, make a cup of tea (admittedly, though, it is often a glass of wine), and get in bed to watch some good TV. Eventually we turn out the lights, settle in, and drift off to sleep. This routine is what we associate with sleep.

What happens if we deviate from this, say, by staying up late for a night out? It's usually harder to fall asleep and our nights are less restful, leaving us tired and foggy the next day. For babies, the bedtime routine you create and the supports that you provide (white noise, lovies, and maybe even pacifiers) are what they will associate with sleep, both when you lay them down for the night or naps *and* when they wake between sleep cycles. The props that babies use to fall asleep aren't necessarily bad habits unless they become a problem, interrupting their ability to fall asleep or back to sleep without the props.

When you are up all night rocking babies or putting binkies back in the crib because your babies aren't able to fall asleep or stay asleep without that sleep association, that's when you may have a problem. Not only are you sleep deprived, but so are your babies.

We aren't saying that rocking, pacifiers, or soothing your babies back to sleep is bad. It is completely natural for parents to answer the cries of their babies and provide them comfort. The difference is that there are ways to provide comforts that probably won't keep everyone up all night. Really, the choice is yours. You have to decide, as the parent, what works for you and what will help ensure that everyone is getting enough restful sleep.

Look for sleep props that your babies like and that help them self-soothe, like lovies that bear your scent (wear them around in your shirt during the day) or white noise. The best thing you can do now is teach your babies how to fall asleep independently so they don't need you when they transition through sleep cycles during the night.

# Before Sleep Scheduling (Weeks 0 to 6)

When babies are born, their sleep is immature, fragmented, and unpredictable. For parents and babies who leave the hospital after a few days, at home you will likely find yourselves feeding around the clock for several weeks. Sleep cycles are still developing and trying to establish a schedule isn't really plausible yet. In the beginning, the schedule may consist of changing diapers, feeding, and laying your babies down to sleep at the same time. As they grow, their periods of awake time will allow for playtime to be added into their schedule, which will later help them differentiate day from night.

If one or more of your babies spend time in the NICU, by the time they come home you may see eating and sleeping patterns emerging thanks to the nurses who cared for them. Caring for multiple babies at once means that NICU nurses will likely be able to get babies on schedules earlier than parents could or are inclined to. While no one hopes their little ones spend time in the NICU, as the testimonials in this chapter show, NICU time can set up parents for an easier time at home with feeding and sleeping once the babies are discharged.

**jenn says**

My nephew was born three months before my twins, and let me tell you, that kid was a champion sleeper. As a result, I had very unrealistic expectations of what newborn sleep looks like. The thing is, some babies will naturally sleep well on their own, while many babies won't. I distinctly remember searching high and low for some magic recipe to help my babies sleep like my nephew did, but the reality is that each baby is different. Some parents get lucky with champion sleepers, but all babies need to be taught healthy sleep habits at some point.

# TIPS FROM A PRO: NIGHTTIME FEEDINGS

*Kelly Wecker, CAPPA-certified postpartum doula and trained newborn sleep specialist*

Babies need to get enough to eat during the day so they can quickly get back to their birth weight and begin sleeping for longer stretches at night, but some newborns can be lethargic during feeding time. To help wake them up so they can eat more efficiently, try taking their clothes off, using a cold cloth, or laying them on a cold, flat surface.

A great option for nighttime feedings that allows parents to get a bit more sleep is this: Once mom has recovered, begin taking shifts at night instead of both parents waking up to take care of the babies. This is a great way for both parents to get some quality sleep. For example, one parent's shift is 8:00 p.m. to 2:00 a.m. and the other takes 2:00 a.m. to 8:00 a.m. Taking shifts can be a little daunting at first but will be made easier if you have a ready-to-go "work station" close by. It makes such a huge difference for tired parents feeding babies alone at night to have everything they need at their fingertips in the room. Here's what to include:

+ A cooler with bottles of breast milk or pre-measured formula bottles
+ A bottle warmer or a Thermos with hot water
+ Burp cloths
+ Swaddle blankets
+ Diapers
+ Wipes
+ Clean pajamas (in case your babies need an outfit after a spit up or diaper change)
+ A Twin Z pillow, bouncy chair, or Pack 'n Play (to safely manage both babies at the same time)

Nursing mothers can follow their nursing routines once they are comfortable without the support of a partner.

Wherever you choose to set up and feed, just make sure each baby is safely angled to allow for easy and comfortable digestion (not laying flat) while you tend to the other baby. If you have an airplane neck pillow, they make a great prop for the bottle while burping the other baby, but blankets and small pillows will work. Always be cautious and careful. Most of all, hang in there—everything gets easier with practice!

# Preparing to Schedule (Weeks 6 and 7)

Between six and seven weeks, babies begin to sleep for shorter periods during the day and longer periods at night. They develop shorter periods of REM sleep and longer periods of non-REM sleep, and therefore their predictable sleeping patterns will begin to develop and sleep scheduling becomes possible.

Most of us think of schedules as referring to a clock. When it comes to newborns, that isn't necessarily helpful. Creating a schedule for two humans who can't tell time will force you to become very dependent on routines. A baby's day is reliant upon age-appropriate awake times and feeding needs. Developing routines around sleeping and feeding (as well as changing and playing) that are consistently implemented at the same times each day will help indicate to your babies what is coming next in their day, thus getting your life with twins on a schedule and generally keeping it on track. As soon as you begin learning your babies' patterns and sleep cues, you will eventually get to a point where you can work out a schedule for your children based on the clock.

## Your Own Readiness

Before you begin the process of developing a reliable schedule for your infants, ask yourself this: Am I ready to do this? Get your game face on. Implementing routines with consistency is 100 percent on you, which means that you can't necessarily fly by the seat of your pants one day and strictly stick to your schedule the next. You are about to teach two little humans an important life skill. Although there will inevitably be hiccups along the way, persistence and commitment are crucial to making positive changes to your babies' otherwise unpredictable sleep habits.

**meghan says**

One piece of advice that I was given and learned the hard way was this: "Whatever you do to help your babies sleep you should be prepared to continue for an entire year." This struck a chord with me when I was using the vibration on their Rock 'n Plays and giving them a WubbaNub pacifier to fall asleep, then picking it up every time they threw it out and started crying. I didn't realize that I was creating sleep associations that I'd have to maintain in order for my boys to sleep. When I did finally realize this, we gave it all up and haven't looked back since.

## Start to Track Your Babies

You're doing double diaper changes, trying to remember who ate what and who pooped when, and now we're going to ask you to keep track of a sleep schedule. No, we're not trying to be cruel, we promise! Writing it all down really is the only way sleep-deprived twin parents can keep anything straight. Once you are ready to establish a sleep schedule for your babies, keeping track of their habits during the day and at night will be vital. Tedious as it may sound, this information will help you see patterns in your babies' feeding and sleeping habits. This will help you determine which times are reasonable for feedings and naps during the day and are in line with your babies' natural inclinations. You will also be able to see improvement over time, which is something to celebrate! Use your schedule tracker (see page 73) or a notebook and write down the following for each of your babies:

+ Morning wake time

+ Feed times and how much or how long the baby ate

- Naps: what time you put them down, how long they slept, and wake time

- Mood upon waking

- Start of bedtime routine and when they actually fell asleep

- Time of night wakings and feedings

## Feeding Considerations

With scheduling, you decide the times when your babies will be fed both during the day and at night. While feeding throughout the day can be time-consuming (not to mention tiring), usually parents are looking to schedule primarily to reduce the number of nighttime feedings and bring predictability to when they are awake in the night. All babies will transition to sleeping longer stretches at night at different rates, but typically babies will begin to require fewer overnight feedings once they double their birth weight and are at least 12 to 14 pounds. Babies should be consuming 28 ounces in a 12-hour period during the day to realistically set them up for longer sleep stretches in the night without compromising their nutritional needs. Of course, it is harder for breast-feeding mothers to pinpoint how many ounces their babies consume each day. According to the website *KellyMom* (a fantastic resource for breastfeeding information for both singleton and twin parents), you will know your babies are getting enough milk when they are:

- Gaining adequate weight

- Producing six or more wet diapers a day

- Producing three or four poopy diapers a day

- Alert and active after a feeding

- Typically meeting developmental milestones

One question we hear a lot is whether formula or breast milk makes a difference when it comes to scheduling feedings, both during the day and at night. The fact of the matter is, formula takes more time and effort for little ones to digest. This means breast-fed babies will likely experience hunger sooner after a prior feeding than formula-fed babies will. To breastfeeding parents, it may feel like it will take more time to get longer stretches of sleep at night—and it might, but that is not necessarily the case; all moms and babies are different. Additionally, research shows that by nine months the difference in sleep patterns between breastfed and bottle-fed babies disappears. There are multiple benefits to breastfeeding or choosing to give your babies breast milk. Ultimately it is your call. When you are ready to begin sleep training, you may want to consider increasing the number of daytime feedings.

### THE DREAM FEED

Once parents begin to be more intentional (and hopeful) about night sleep, many choose to give the babies a dream feed. As we mentioned in the previous chapter (page 111), the dream feed typically occurs between 10 p.m. and 12 a.m., just as parents are heading to bed themselves. Parents wake babies just enough to give them a feeding boost, with the intention of helping parents and babies get through a longer stretch of sleep in the night. The jury is out on the effectiveness of this approach, with some parents having had success while others have not. If you're not comfortable waking your sleeping babies, make sure they get the calories you would deliver via a dream feed earlier in the evening.

Remember that sleeping all night without needing to eat is a developmental milestone much like crawling or walking. Over time these additional nighttime feedings will taper off as your babies' bodies learn to efficiently store calories, but this will vary for each baby. A nighttime feeding can disappear as late as at nine to 12 months, although that isn't usually the norm.

# TWINCREDIBLE

*Paige, mother of Elise and Miles (4 months)*

Getting twins on the same sleep schedule was a roller coaster of highs and lows, and it was easy to get frustrated when they woke up at different times. But then I had an epiphany that completely shifted my perspective. When my daughter was consistently waking up at 5 a.m., bright eyed and ready to start the day, I began to see it as special one-on-one time with her. I would rock her while I drank tea, and we'd watch the sunrise together. Meanwhile, her twin brother decided he would take really short naps in the afternoon. But those became the moments when he had my full attention to practice tummy time and get showered with kisses. Off-schedule sleep became bonding opportunities. And what could have been moments of frustration over not getting more sleep or not getting a break have become some of my most cherished memories.

## Sleep Environment

What makes you comfortable when you sleep? When your sleep environment changes, say, because a light is flipped on or your window slammed shut and it's too hot, you wake up, right? Your babies will resist sleep or wake up more frequently if their sleep environment isn't just right. To encourage babies to learn healthy sleep habits, take a few things into account to make their nursery the ideal environment for sleep.

**Temperature.** If the nursery isn't at a good temperature or the babies are dressed too warmly, they will have a harder time getting comfortable.

The temperatures in your babies' nursery should ideally range from 68 to 72 degrees Fahrenheit. With the temperature in that range, your twins should only need one layer of pajamas with a sleep sack or swaddle, never any additional blankets.

**White noise.** We mentioned white noise machines in the gear chapter and again touched on it as an important part of establishing a sleep routine earlier in this chapter. By now it's no surprise that we think they're very helpful in creating an ideal sleep environment.

White noise machines simulate the comforting noises of the womb and drown out any household noises that could potentially wake the babies up. We understand that the inclusion of white noise machines is a personal preference, but know that their use doesn't necessarily create a negative sleep association. The noise can be a soothing constant that you don't have to constantly recreate for your babies.

**Transitional objects.** While newborns should not sleep with anything in the crib, transitional objects can be both safe and useful with infants who are 6 weeks or older. A transitional object might be a small stuffed animal, lovie, or soft book. The goal is for your child to seek comfort from it, not you, at bedtime and if waking in the night when it's not a scheduled feeding time. What you want to avoid is getting into a situation where you and only you can get your babies back to sleep, either by rocking, replacing a pacifier, or who knows what other tricks you might try (and believe us, tired parents will try anything!). You're working toward more restful sleep for you *and* your babies, which means that your babies need to learn ways to comfort themselves in your absence. This is why you may want to consider a transitional object. We always suggest that parents check the safety of the transitional objects they are considering with their pediatrician.

jenn says

This might sound crazy, but my postpartum doula suggested that I shove the lovies we had bought for our twins in my bra to wear them around for a while, purely so the blankets would absorb my unique mommy smell and be a source of comfort when I placed them in the cribs. I eventually snuggled their lovies between us while we nursed and cuddled, which I believe allowed my children to develop a positive association with them, ultimately helping them settle themselves to sleep. A word to the wise, however, I have learned from experience to buy more than one of the items you choose to be your transitional objects and give them some love. Having an extra on hand, in case of damage or loss, will be your saving grace!

## Together or Separate?

Ah, the twin-related conundrums that you never really consider until you're faced with parenting two babies. Should my twins share a crib? A room? Our experiences took two different paths, with one of us putting our twins in the same crib for some time and one of us splitting up the babies from the beginning. Sleeping arrangements are a personal preference and will vary for each family. If you do decide to have your twins share a crib, understand all the precautions you should take against SIDS and know when it is an appropriate time to split them up. (See Resources, page 161, for links to sites with excellent educational information about SIDS.) Consider assigning a certain side of the crib to each baby to help develop consistency and routine for your twins.

Though it may be hard to believe, typically infant twins won't wake each other up during the night. They get very used to each other's noises. But if you notice that your twins are waking each other up throughout the night while sharing a sleeping space, you may want to consider alternative sleeping arrangements. There is more information about twins sharing a crib at TwoCameTrue.com.

Once you are ready to start scheduling sleep, it may help if you give them their own sleeping spaces. While we don't always suggest that parents separate their twins into different rooms, some families do decide that it works best for them. This, again, is a decision for what works best for parents, the configuration of their homes, and even their lifestyle. If the twins are in separate rooms and your schedule has you doing a nighttime feed (or two), keep in mind that each room will need some furniture for you to administer a feeding, unless you bring one twin into the room where the other is for feedings.

## IT WORKED FOR US

*Molly and Jeff, parents of Madison and Jameson (12 months)*

When it comes to sleeping, you can read all of the advice in the world, but ultimately do what you need to do! We ended up sleeping in separate beds with one baby each (something we originally said we'd *never* do). At around seven months, Jameson started sleeping through the night for about 10 hours—he just figured it out. From 9½ months to 11 months Madison started waking up every two hours to eat. After a sleep-deprived "ah-ha" moment, we figured out that she didn't need the bottle, she just wanted us. Two nights of crying it out (never more than 30 minutes) and she, too, figured out how to sleep through the night.

# Scheduling Sleep (Weeks 7 to 8)

Around seven or eight weeks, begin establishing bedtime routines and making a point of teaching your babies to fall asleep independently at nap times and at night. If your babies were premature, you might want to use their adjusted age to help you determine when they might be ready to be on a set schedule. Twins who arrive early typically weigh less and might require more frequent feeding. As a result, it will take them a little longer to be ready for a sleep schedule, and the timing will depend on how many weeks premature they were.

To prepare the babies for sleep scheduling:

+ Introduce a predictable and consistent bedtime routine.

+ Cluster feed: Give your babies the opportunity to nurse several times within the hour or two before bedtime.

+ Consider introducing a 10:00 p.m. or 11:00 p.m. dream feed (see page 130).

- Keep the room dark with white noise, and dress your babies appropriately to encourage longer stretches of sleep.

- Remember that night waking in breastfed babies is considered normal but temporary.

## Set a Schedule

Once you begin to see more predictability in your babies' eating and sleeping habits, set a schedule and stick to it! Setting a schedule means providing basic care for your infants at the same time. Each day, you'll stick to the predetermined time for when the babies are fed or laid down to sleep. We recommend doing everything for your twins at the same time, even if that means waking a sleeping baby. The foundation of your schedule will be age-appropriate waking and feeding intervals, as well as the routines that you develop around those activities.

As we've already explained (but it's worth a reminder), there are many benefits to setting a schedule for your babies—your sanity included—but the most important is that babies thrive on predictability and do best when they know what is coming next in their day. When schedules work, they ensure that babies are well-rested.

By using the schedule tracker, patterns will emerge around when your babies typically eat and sleep at this point in their lives. While they may have needed to eat every one to three hours in the weeks after coming home from the hospital, by this point you might notice that your feedings have stretched to every three hours, or perhaps four. Being aware of details like these will allow you to set a schedule for the babies that reflects what their bodies are doing naturally. On the following page is a sample schedule that has worked for many twins parents.

## SAMPLE SCHEDULE

+ 7 a.m. feed

+ 11 a.m. feed

+ 3 p.m. feed

+ 7 p.m. bedtime feed

+ 11 p.m. feed

+ 3 a.m. feed

+ 7 a.m. feed

## The Twin Challenge

Of course, even though babies will benefit from scheduling, that doesn't mean they won't test you as you try to implement it. We have to warn you that it won't necessarily be easy. Teaching one baby how to sleep is challenging, let alone two! The added twist twin parents have is dealing with nighttime wakings when they don't happen simultaneously.

What happens when one twin wakes before a scheduled feeding in the middle of the night? You might feel inclined to feed a baby off schedule so you can go back to bed for one more hour. But before you break down, so soon after starting, remember this: The instant gratification you get from that hour of sleep doesn't do you or the babies a favor in the long run. When one of the babies wakes at 6:00 a.m., an hour ahead of the scheduled feeding, distract him with toys, songs, or books. Put the baby in a sling or carrier or walk through different rooms of the house so that you can buy time until your regularly scheduled feeding. While it may be hard in the moment (and who are we kidding, it *will* be hard), sticking to your schedule will get everyone in sync, making your life that much more manageable.

As time goes on, ideally you'll see the night wakings push later and later. When this happens, work to move the feeding schedule later into the night by not feeding either baby until the second baby wakes. For example, again using the sample schedule on the previous page, if your babies typically wake at 3 a.m., but baby B has started to sleep through that feeding to, say, 3:15, feed both babies at 3:15. The next night, you will feed the babies at 3:15 am at the very earliest, again holding off until the second baby wakes. Working in this fashion you will eventually get to the point where your babies will no longer wake to eat.

Don't forget: As you reduce the frequency of night feedings and work to eliminate them altogether, you are simply redistributing calories from the nighttime feedings to the daytime feedings. You aren't reducing the amount your babies eat, you're just shifting the times when those calories are eaten.

## IT WORKED FOR US

*Samantha and Jeff, parents of Cade and Quinn (7 years)*

At five months, we saw a clear pattern that our son, Cade, was a consistent sleeper, while his sister was taking a bit longer to find her rhythm. Quinn would wake Cade nightly so we decided to separate them into different rooms. Instinctually, this seemed like the best way to at least get Cade his sleep while we helped Quinn.

After six months of sleeping separately, Quinn continued to struggle. I began to reflect on my own youth as a twin and how, despite our having our own rooms, my twin sister and I chose to sleep side by side. So we decided to try them in one room again, and what we found was that Quinn needed her brother. They would lie quietly looking at each other from their independent cribs and this brought comfort to Quinn. Pushing past our own fears of sleepless nights and instead letting the twins organically connect, bond, and soothe each other as they fall asleep still works for them today.

# What to Expect

Teaching babies to sleep is notoriously hard work. If babies slept peacefully straight out of the womb, cooed happily, and easily drifted off to sleep, parents wouldn't be so famously tired. Set realistic expectations for your babies and for yourself.

## Crying

If you decide to use a sleep schedule before your babies are able to fall asleep independently, you can anticipate a challenge when putting them to bed for the night. Laying your babies down drowsy but awake can be as simple as following your usual bedtime routine, spending the last 15 minutes of that time soothing your babes to a drowsy state, and then laying them down before they are fully asleep. Then, give your last goodnight kisses, and walk out of their nursery. If they protest, don't

## When Good Sleepers Stop Sleeping

There are several factors that can contribute to babies' sleep falling off. Illness, teething, cognitive milestones, regressions, travel, and even the time change can all affect how your babies sleep. The good news is these things are temporary. When these hiccups arise, try to troubleshoot the best that you can, and remember that this, too, shall pass. Do your best to soothe and love your babies during these changes, but try not to use bad habits to bandage the bumps. By no means are we saying you should throw out the window everything you have taught your babies. What we want you to know is that you need to give yourself permission to be flexible and work through setbacks in a way that is realistic.

go rushing in immediately, but rather give them a few minutes to try and settle themselves. After as little as a minute or two, you can go in and gently pat their backs until the crying stops. The key here is not to pick them up, make eye contact, or talk to them. Pat, shush, and leave again once they are settled. It will take time for the learning to take place and at times might feel like it's hopeless, but with practice and consistency, your twins *will* learn to soothe themselves and fall asleep independently.

The goal of sleep scheduling, at least in our minds, is to introduce predictability into the day and night and prepare babies for regular feeding and waking times. It isn't to let your babies cry until they just figure it out or get what they want. For a baby, crying is their way to communicate that they aren't happy with the situation, but there are comforts you can offer other than a bottle or breast to end crying spells as quickly as possible and let you babies know you're there for them. Remember that shushing, allowing babies to suck (on a finger or pacifier, not a bottle or breast), and swaddling are simple ways to settle babies when they're upset.

**Expert mom tip:** *Babies crying, pausing for a few moments, and then crying again can be taken as a sign that they are learning. You may think they are just tired and taking a breath, but in fact they are figuring out that if they cry, someone comes to get them, or if they cry, they get fed. Everyone in this situation is learning.*

## One Baby Adapting More Quickly

Twins may share a birthday and a womb, but your twins are unique individuals. It is not uncommon for twin parents to have one baby who rides the wave of feeding and sleeping schedules more easily than the other. It's also incredibly normal to feel frustrated by this. Patience. Pause and recognize the individual successes of each of your babies and remember that each will find their groove in due time.

## Sleep Regressions

There are four different times when babies experience sleep regressions in the first two years of life. Some babies may show few signs of regression and others will leaving you wondering where in the world your sweet sleeper ran off to. Although challenging to your sanity, sleep regressions are short lived and only occur because of the babies' cognitive and physical development. Understanding when and why you may encounter sleep challenges throughout infancy will help you feel prepared and capable of getting through it. And as long as you avoid Band-Aiding the problem with bad sleep habits, you will all soon be back to peaceful nights!

**4 months:** A baby's circadian rhythm is more developed and babies are sleeping less like newborns. Parents generally feel that this is the most challenging sleep regression because they had begun to see longer stretches of sleep and then are suddenly plagued by waking up every two to three hours again. Be cognizant of age-appropriate wake times and avoid overtired babies. Work diligently to establish consistent routines.

**8 to 10 months:** Gross motor skills and cognitive developments mean that babies are generally getting ready to drop a nap.

**12 to 15 months:** Learning to walk can affect babies' sleep because they are excited about their newfound freedom.

**Terrible twos:** This is likely the last sleep regression you'll see and comes thanks to the independence that toddlers love to assert.

# Weaning from Nighttime Feedings

After you've been implementing your schedule for some time and it's working, you may start to dream about weaning your babies from nighttime feedings with the hope of them sleeping through the night.

The goal with weaning is to redistribute the calories your babies consume during nighttime feedings to the daytime feedings so that, in total, they are not consuming any less. Tracking your babies' habits will be really helpful in reallocating the ounces consumed at night to daytime feedings, so let us reiterate that you don't want to skip the tracking step.

Using our sample schedule (page 136), you will see that nighttime feedings happened at 11 p.m. and 3 a.m. Here's how to approach weaning with that schedule:

+ Work to eliminate the latest feeding (3 a.m.) first, dispersing those eliminated nighttime ounces evenly into your daytime feedings. If you are bottle feeding, reducing the amount by a half ounce every three days or so. For breastfeeding, reduce the time you nurse by two minutes about every three days.

+ Continue to repeat this pattern until you have successfully ditched the 3 a.m. feeding for good. Expect that your babies might make progress at different rates.

+ Once the middle of the night feeding is gone and your waking at that hour has stopped rather consistently, repeat the same approach with with the next nighttime feeding (using the sample, the 11 p.m. dream feed).

If your babies wake after you have eliminated a feeding, try to let them self-soothe and put themselves back to sleep. If that isn't successful, help out and stop the fussing but remember to keep your interactions minimal, with little to no talking. Eventually, with your support and continued practice with putting them down drowsy but awake, they will be able to put themselves back to sleep.

# Sleep Training

Sleep training is a hot topic that has parents sitting on both sides of the fence. This book may be your first introduction to sleep training, or perhaps you have some familiarity with buzzwords such as "Ferberized" and "cry it out." Whether you decide to move past sleep scheduling to sleep training is a deeply personal choice. Know that you have options when it comes to training your twins to sleep through the night. We have offered sleep consultations services to numerous twin parents and understand that many parents seek a customized approach. Here we'll describe some of the most common approaches to sleep training that you can implement yourself. Know that if the going gets truly tough, there are professionals you can hire to work with you over e-mail, video conferencing, or in your home to help your babies learn to sleep through the night.

When it comes to sleep training, there isn't a one-size-fits-all approach. Professionals have developed numerous theories and methods, giving families the opportunity to choose those that fit best with their lifestyle and parenting philosophies. Next we'll walk through five of the most common sleep training methods that parents of singletons and multiples alike typically consider. Keep in mind that, to successfully tackle sleep training your twins, you should be adequately recovered from their birth and feeling healthy and mentally prepared for crying spells (potentially yours as well as the babies'!) and some long, yet short-lived, nights.

**Extinction ("cry it out"):** This method was developed by Dr. Marc Weissbluth, a pediatrician. The idea behind extinction is that parents will lovingly implement a soothing and consistent bedtime routine, lay their baby down drowsy but awake, and then leave the bedroom. If one or both babies protest (cry), the parents let them work it out on their own without parental intervention. Many parents are uncomfortable with the thought of letting their babies cry until they fall asleep, so you'll need to decide together whether this approach is right for your family. Weissbluth is the author of the twin-specific sleep book *Healthy Sleep Habits, Happy Twins*. He outlines an approach to sleep with twins, which begins long before the actual period of sleep training to set babies up for success with extinction.

**Graduated extinction** (Check and console, or the Ferber method): The most well-known version of graduated extinction was developed by Dr. Richard Ferber, founder and former director of the Center for Pediatric Sleep Disorders at Children's Hospital in Boston. With Ferber's method, the goal is for babies to put themselves to sleep when and if they wake without the help of the parents. At the initial bedtime, parents lay the babies down drowsy but awake and then leave the room. The goal of his method is not to help your baby fall asleep but simply to reassure them that you are nearby. The method has parents plan for several check-ins with their babies, if needed, and console crying babies without picking them up, usually by patting and shushing. The time between checks should increase slightly each time a check-in is needed, and this is why the extinction is referred to as *graduated*. So, for example, the first check-in might happen two minutes after the parents leave the room. After leaving, if crying persists, the next check-in will happen five minutes later, and so on in increasing intervals. Ferber outlines his sleep method in the book *Solve Your Child's Sleep Problems*.

**The chair method:** While you can anticipate some crying with this method, it doesn't require you to leave your babies in the room alone. As with the prior methods, parents will perform the babies' bedtime routine as usual and lay the babies down drowsy but awake. Instead of leaving, one parent will sit in the room near the cribs (whether you use a chair is up to you). The parent should remain quiet and not give the babies attention. The purpose of your presence in the room is to reassure the babies that they are not alone. Gradually, you move farther and farther away from the crib until you are no longer in the room. Because the movement is gradual, it may take a couple of weeks, rather than a handful of days, for you to feel comfortable leaving the room entirely.

**Pick up, put down:** This is a gentler method of sleep training that can be used with babies as young as 6 to 8 weeks old. The initial approach is still the same—lay your babies down drowsy but awake and leave the room. If crying starts, parents wait and listen for a minute or two. If crying persists, one parent returns to the room and picks up the crying baby (or both parents enter if both babies are crying) to soothe or console them until they are in a drowsy state, at which point the baby or babies are set back in the crib to fall asleep. This routine is repeated as necessary until the babies fall asleep. Keep in mind that it can require a bit of patience from the parents, as babies may resume their crying with multiple put-downs before finally falling asleep. And some babies, depending on their temperament, can become more stimulated by being picked up, which may lengthen the amount of time it takes to get them back to sleep.

**Fade it out:** This is also a very gentle method of training babies to fall a sleep independently that can be used with babies between 6 and 8 weeks old. Here parents fade out the sleep supports that babies may need (such as feeding to sleep or rocking) over time. Because those scaffolds are removed slowly your babies gradually learn to do the work of putting themselves to sleep independently. This method is for those willing to put in longer-term effort, as our little ones often doggedly resist losing the comforts of rocking or falling asleep while feeding. However, it's great for parents who don't want crying to play a role in their sleep training efforts.

## Five Common Sleep Training Hiccups

Regardless of the approach they choose, even the most strong-willed parents will have moments of weakness when in the throes of sleep training. These are the slips twin parents most commonly live to regret:

**Having bad timing.** Starting before your babies are cognitively and physically ready; while they are sick; while they are working through other transitions like moving into their crib; or while you have visitors will not set you up for a successful sleep training experience. Although you are exhausted, wait until everything is just right.

**Letting the babies nap on the go.** While it is helpful and convenient for parents to let their babies sleep in the car or stroller, it can become a negative sleep association. Babies can become accustomed to the movement and eventually struggle to sleep when the earth isn't moving underneath them.

**Rocking the babies just this one time.** The number one thing that you need to sustain is consistency, even when it feels too damn hard to do. The one time you decide to rock them to sleep or put the pacifier back will undo much of your hard work.

**Skipping a nap or letting the babies stay up too late.** Overtired babies don't fall asleep easily or stay asleep. While you are laying the foundation for good sleepers, be diligent about following your nap and bedtime schedule.

**Starting and stopping, then starting and stopping again.** We get it. Parents go into sleep training with the best of intentions to get through it so they can start sleeping for long stretches again. And then an off night happens and they decide to throw it to the wind and try again later. Too many "false starts" teach the babies that they will eventually get out of having to learn what you are trying to teach them. When you decide to start teaching your babies healthy sleep habits—whether you are simply syncing schedules or diving into sleep training—commit to it 100 percent, even when it feels really hard.

# 7

# Parenting
# as a Team

In one way, shape, or form, you brought these two babies into this world together. Your journey over the last months—from becoming pregnant and learning that you were carrying two babies to coming to grips with the reality that you are expected to keep them alive—may have rocked your world a bit. There may be challenges from time to time as you learn to successfully parent twins as a cohesive unit, but your bond with your partner can be immeasurably strengthened by these two little additions to your family. Ultimately, your most important job as a parent is to shower your children with love while molding them into kind, well-mannered humans.

## Align Your Parenting Styles

When push comes to shove, 90 percent of good parenting simply means that you are showing up. Ultimately, your job is to love, nurture, and guide your children through life, molding them into the type of people that you hope and dream they will become. Parenting is like a dance: It is at its most beautiful when you follow the music, letting it lead you. The best dancers trust their partners to take the reins when it feels right, and even when they don't seem to feel the rhythm, let them dance like they've never danced before.

Speaking of dance, are you more hip hop and your partner more jazz? Pause for a moment while you each consider your own upbringing. How does your childhood differ from your partner's? There are parts of your childhood that you will value as you parent your own children and other parts that you can live without.

The time you spend aligning who you want to be as parents is invaluable. Children thrive in consistent environments where they can expect the same response from both of their parents. Kids will be kids, trying to finagle their way around the decision each parent makes, but when parents work as a team, kids learn valuable lessons about the solidarity that should exist in a healthy relationship.

Ultimately, raising children forces us to take an in-depth look at our own beliefs or why we are the way we are. Being stuck in your ways or working against each other only creates polarizing tension in a household, which makes it tougher for your marriage and your children to thrive.

## IT WORKED FOR US

*Paige, mother of Elise and Miles (4 months) and Brice (3 years)*

When we had just one child, I got into the bad habit of trying to do everything on my own. But once we had twins and a toddler? It was *all* hands on deck. And it's completely transformed our relationship into a partnership. We figured out which tasks we each prefer and began dividing and conquering. My husband is great at thinking ahead, so he preps anything I might not be able to do throughout the day. That includes making breakfast, snacks, and lunch for all of us (especially since nursing twins has me eating like a linebacker) and giving our toddler breakfast while I feed the babies. We also tag team on the chores. I meal plan while he grocery shops on the weekends. He starts laundry that I (sometimes) finish during the day. Getting clear on who is doing what each week and saying yes to every offer of help has made a huge difference, because the only thing more incredible than having twins is the amount of laundry that comes with them!

# Have Each Other's Backs

Yes, your job is to care for your new bundles of joy, but just as importantly, your job is to continue to look out for each other. Either parent may have difficulties coping or may be surprised by how postpartum depression (PPD) can sneak into your life. Periodically take a moment for a mental health check (referring back to our tips in chapter 2), for yourself *and* your partner. Remember that there is no shame in struggling to adjust to your new role. As a parenting team, presume positive intentions, and know that the intention is to help each other, not cast blame.

Your life with kids is not going to look the same as it did before they were born. You both have to be able to accept that and make adjustments. Find systems that work in your home where you both participate. Go with your partner's approach in a given situation with the twins, even if it might not be how you'd approach it yourself. See what happens. Sharing the load helps ensure one person isn't carrying all of the weight. Life will begin to function pretty seamlessly when you explicitly make a plan *together* that tackles the changes that parenting brings.

This is all great training for later, when the twins will really test you as a team. When one parent says no, what do kids naturally do? They go find their other parent, hoping that the answer might change. Parenting is sometimes hard, can challenge us to the core, and can easily leave us feeling deflated. Your partner is your teammate, so rely on each other to be a support and back up. If at times you feel like you are on opposite sides of the fence, discuss your different perspectives when you are away from the children as you seek a supportive, if not a unified, way forward.

## Journaling Opportunity

Before you sit down to have a conversation with each other, use this journaling opportunity to gain some clarity about your parenting ideals. Then use your responses to have an honest discussion about your team parenting style.

*I believe a good parent is*

_____

_____

_____

_____

_____

*It is important that our children are*

_____

_____

_____

_____

_____

*As a parent, I see myself as*

_____

_____

_____

_____

*My goal as a parent is*

_____

_____

_____

_____

*Discipline is*

_____

_____

_____

_____

After years of experience as an educator, I felt confident and I loved the feeling of being able to help kids learn how to read, even in the most difficult of circumstances. Then I became a parent, and holy moly, I suddenly felt like a new teacher all over again, navigating uncharted waters. I had to really dig deep into my own childhood to find what I valued as a parent. Since those early days, I have found my stride and can now hold my head high. Becoming a new parent is a humbling experience. There is a lot to learn, and that learning curve is pretty damn steep. Keep your chin up. You may feel like you are flailing, but to your partner, to others, and, most important, to your children . . . you are a superhero.

# Always Assume Positive Intent

Without sugarcoating it, the truth is that parents can become exhausted and overworked. Sometimes that's just part of the job description. The thing to always keep in your mind is that you are both doing your very best for your babies. Sometimes, decisions may be made by one of you in the middle of the night or in the other's absence—not to exclude either of you from parenting, but because you are a team. If you have come together at some point to align your beliefs and your goals, you can safely assume that each other's intentions are good.

## Be Prepared for a Piece of Humble Pie Every Now and Then

There are a lot of resources out there that can teach you how to parent by giving you advice on what to do and what not to do. However, it's unfair to expect perfection, because raising kids means having curveballs thrown at you almost daily. The best we can do as parents is to reflect, find a way to accept being wrong every now and then, and say sorry.

Find those parenting wins and bank them in your memory. You will have moments of self-doubt. You will likely learn a lesson or two in humility as a twin parent, because of the simple fact that you have a lot to juggle. Don't be too hard on yourself or your partner.

## Use "I" Statements

As parents, tired and challenged by the give and take that parenting requires, there are bound to be disagreements. Emotional explosions can and will happen. In those moments, throwing accusations at each other might feel like a satisfying solution, but it will only damage you as a team. However, stating out loud how *you* feel isn't accusing anyone. By talking honestly and openly, you might be able to find a resolution to lessen your frustration with each other. And by using "I feel" statements, the person on the receiving end will most likely be less defensive because blame is not being placed directly on them.

**meghan says**

Nobody ever died from telling someone how they feel. We give each other the right to express how we feel, without judgment. My husband and I follow this philosophy when we have to have difficult conversations. Ultimately, your feelings are really just that—feelings. You are 100 percent allowed to feel any which way you want. When I hold back because I just don't want to have a long and maybe challenging discussion, my husband tunes in and says, "Nobody ever died." Those words put us in a neutral zone where either one of us can just talk, and we establish a space to hear each other out.

## Don't Take Things Too Seriously

Yes, raising kids is serious business. You are now responsible for keeping two people alive *and* molding them into good people. That *is* a lot. By no means are we trying to downplay the importance of your role here, but we do think that keeping a sense of humor is worth mentioning. There will be many moments that are definitely worth a good laugh.

We made a pact early on to be open and honest with our parenting mistakes. One morning when I was out of town, my husband called and burst into laughter as he told me about his dad fail. The night before, he put the kids to bed and then lay down to watch some TV before going to sleep himself. Well, around 2 a.m. he woke up to find the TV on and the kids in bed with him. They had snuck into his room while he was sound asleep, crawled into bed, and enjoyed some TV. While these moments aren't always our proudest, they are priceless memories of our lives together as a family, which is why we add them to our memory bank. Thanks to so many of these moments, we began keeping a memory jar, filled with sticky notes recording funny things our kids have said and stories just like this one.

## IT WORKED FOR US

*Julia and Kyle, parents of Jackson and Luke (18 months)*

My husband and I are lucky enough for me to be able to be at home full time with our twin boys. It is an understatement to say that by the end of the day we are both exhausted from our jobs. One night my husband had an idea: "Let's play 'call your baby.'" The rules are simple: When your partner gets home from the day they name the twin that will be their responsibility for the night. For example, Kyle would come home and say, "I call Luke," and from that point on all feeding, bathing, changing, etc. for Luke would be in Kyle's hands. One exception is playtime because that is a family affair. It might not seem like it would offer much of a break, but for those few hours it really did. I wasn't going in circles in charge of all kid duties. We also got some quality one-on-one time with each twin. Usually the next night we would switch, so our love and time were spread equally to each baby.

# Keeping the Love Alive

Trying to keep your relationship thriving without kids is hard, never mind throwing a few tiny humans into the mix. Those first few weeks after birth might seem longer because of the demands of pumping, feeding, and diaper changing, but once you come up for a breath, the clouds will part. A date will be calling your name, and we're here to tell you that dating after the babies are born is completely possible.

These dates don't have to be fancy nights out on the town; just make them regular and deliberate. This is kid-free time together and can happen with or without a babysitter. When we can't find a sitter, we still block off time on our calendar and have date night in our living room once the kids fall asleep. It doesn't have to be with romantic lighting—you'd probably fall asleep! Just turn off the technology, order a pizza, and have a glass of wine or a beer. It'll feel really good to catch up, sans babies.

Relationships are a ton of fun but also work. Laughing over the funny stuff your twins did or secretly flirting behind the kitchen counter is fun. Your life as a new couple parenting twins can at times be chaotic, but your partner is the last person to console you at night, has those 3 a.m. conversations about the things that make you lose sleep, and is the first person to impact your life the next morning. Even in less-than-stellar moments, cherish that person. In a way, having two babies at home could be compared with the pre-baby bar scene days. It's noisy, you won't want to know what you just stepped on, and someone might occasionally puke. Perspective, right? Enjoy being a couple and take everything in stride; this is a short season in life.

## Partnership Affirmations

- Remember why you chose each other in the first place
- Make sure your parenting goals are aligned
- Assume good intentions
- Make time for your other children
- Make time for the two of you
- Take care of each other

**jenn says**

Learning to manage life with two little ones complicated our life as a couple. Although we thought we had everything planned out during pregnancy, we found ourselves tired, inexperienced, vulnerable, and sometimes wanting to chuck bottles at each other. A few months into our new adventure, a dear friend "forced" us to let her babysit. That night gave us the opportunity to look each other in the eyes, organically reconnect, and talk. Without our two sweet babies constantly chirping at us, we finally openly communicated and were able to get things straight between us. We remembered why we chose each other and we figured out how to align ourselves as parents.

# Making Time for Other Children

Welcoming twins into your family is a big adjustment, not only for parents but for older siblings as well. To help ease the transition for your other children, we often remind parents to have a deliberate conversation with each other and define how you will ensure everyone in the family gets enough attention once the twins are home. Together, or with your children involved, identify simple ways to give kids individual attention, like going for a walk or a trip to Target during naptime, or maybe even having a special dinner together once the twins are in bed.

# IT WORKED FOR US

*Christina and Chris, parents of Nilsy and Ryan (3 years)*
*and Sawyer (5 years)*

Having multiples has made me a bit more of a control freak (of the few things I can control). I am all for fostering independence, but now I plan and organize all the kids' clothes on the weekend for the week ahead. This started when the twins were a few months old and my husband was going away for a week. I thought this would make it easier to get my oldest to school, and now I can't live without planning everything out meticulously. My oldest puts in his requests, but this little task makes mornings and nighttime routines much easier, especially if we have plans. I set out pajamas for each day, too. If there is a theme day at school or something out of the ordinary, I know what needs to be clean and ready in advance. While this isn't for everyone, the work I put in on the weekend eases my mind. Some people meal prep, but for this mom of twins plus one, clothes prep is my life saver.

# Making Time for Yourself

At one point in your life you probably had a social calendar filled with cocktail hours and weekend getaways. Your friendships and the life you led when you were single are a part of who you are. Friendships are a fundamental piece of your life, and maintaining them now is vitally important. It can be easy to get swept up in your role as a parent and a partner, which is why you should give each other some space to find enjoyment and an identity outside of the home. Sometimes in those short absences, you appreciate each other so much more.

# In Closing

So, do you feel ready? We hope that we have given you a well-stocked parenting toolbox that will help you feel prepared as your two babies arrive, as well as reminded you that reaching out for help—be it for practical household to-dos, mental health, or medical support—is *perfectly okay!* When things get challenging, remember that you are a team—two people who can create harmony by being open with each other—and approach your parenting in the same way. Forming a unified team will ultimately create more time for yourself, each other, and everyone else in your family. As you close up these pages, our hope is that you walk away feeling like your life has some semblance of order even in the midst of the beautiful chaos that raising twins produces.

Of course, our jobs as parents are never done, so while your parenting journey is just beginning, we are still navigating parenthood every day, finding what works and what doesn't. Feel free to reach out to us when your parenting journey takes a turn and you need a supportive village. Until we meet again!

# Resources

Since welcoming our own twins into the world and subsequently creating our online community, which connects and supports fellow twin parents all over the world, we have come across some incredible parenting resources that we feel every parent needs to have in their back pocket. Although resources for parents of multiples are easier to come by these days, we are including our favorites for you to peruse.

## Books

+ **Multiples Illuminated**, by Megan Woolsey and Alison Lee. *Multiples Illuminated* brings parents real-life stories and helpful advice related to infertility, coping with pregnancy, labor and delivery, the NICU, breastfeeding, and surviving the infancy and toddlerhood.

+ **Healthy Sleep Habits, Happy Twins**, by Marc Weissbluth, MD. This is a great guide for sleep training multiples written by a pediatrician and renowned sleep authority.

+ **Dad's Guide to Raising Twins**, by Joe Rawlinson. This book contains helpful advice for dads or nonpregnant parents to help them survive twin pregnancy and prepare for raising twins.

+ **When You're Expecting Twins, Triplets, or Quads**, by Dr. Barbara Luke, Tamara Eberlein, and Dr. Roger B. Newman. This book is filled with practical guidelines to help maintain a healthy pregnancy.

## Websites and Blogs

+ **TwoCameTrue.com.** This is our own blog, where we share personal stories and write helpful articles aimed at supporting twin families as they navigate life with multiples, from pregnancy to parenting school-aged twins.

+ **Sidelines.org.** This is a wonderfully supportive community for women experiencing high-risk pregnancies, bed rest, and premature birth.

+ **BabySleepSite.com.** Started by a mom inspired by her own children's sleep challenges, this site is run by an expert team of sleep consultants. You can find everything from free resources to a members-only library and customized consulting services.

+ **KellyMom.com.** This site was developed by an international board-certified lactation consultant and mom of three to be a place to find evidence-based information on breastfeeding and parenting.

+ **DadsGuideToTwins.com.** This site is run by Joe Rawlinson, a twin father, and is a great place for dads to find twin-parenting resources and support of their own. He has authored two helpful books as well, one of which is recommended on the previous page.

+ **RaisingMultiples.org.** *Raising Multiples* is the leading national non-profit provider of support, education, and research on multiple births. They advocate for quality prenatal care and healthy deliveries and supply information to all multiple-birth families to support successful parenting of multiples.

+ **MultiplesOfAmerica.org.** *Multiples of America* is dedicated to providing families of multiples with support, education, and research. They partner with local support groups, health care providers, researchers, and educators to help parents of multiples.

+ **PregnantChicken.com.** This is a place to learn all about pregnancy and newborns, with a realistic perspective and sense of humor.

+ **MamasOfTheNICU.org.** *Mamas of the NICU* is a supportive community that helps parents with children in the NICU by connecting them with NICU graduate families as mentors. Founder Bianca Dottin is also the author of *Mommy's NICU Journal*, in which parents can document every step of their NICU journey.

## Children's Books

+ **Fraturtles**, by Keith Greenstein. This is a great book to help teach kids that being a twin isn't about sharing their looks, but rather sharing their lives.

+ **God Gave Us Two**, by Lisa Tawn Bergren and Laura J. Bryant. This is a great book for families with children who are expecting two new siblings, affirming that a parent's love won't change.

+ **The Twinniest Twins**, by Amy Kuhr and Natalya Pilavci. This is all about how twins are as different as they are the same. A portion of book sales goes to ProjectNightNight.org, which supports children living in homelessness.

+ **Twice Upon a Time**, by Lynn Lorenz. This is a set of baby memory books written especially for parents of twins.

+ **Two Is for Twins**, by Wendy Cheyette Lewison and Hiroe Nakata. This celebrates the joys of "twindom."

## More Information

**CO-BEDDING TWINS**

✛ www.parenting.com/article/can-twins-share-a-crib

✛ www.ncbi.nlm.nih.gov/pmc/articles/PMC3496289/

**POSTPARTUM SUPPORT**

✛ Postpartum Support International Warmline 1-800-944-4773

✛ www.Postpartum.net

✛ www.PostpartumProgress.com

**SIDS**

✛ www.cdc.gov/sids/AboutSUIDandSIDS.htm

**SLEEP SCHEDULING**

✛ www.sleep.org/articles/breastfeeding-vs-bottle-sleep/

# Index

# Acknowledgments

 Thank you to my steadfast partner in life, Jordan—my husband, my rock, and my friend. Your never-failing love and encouragement make me pinch myself just to be sure our life together isn't a dream. Thank you for being a true partner in parenthood, for keeping your cool when I lose mine, and for embracing our imperfections along the way. And for keeping that napkin!

Dominic and Matteo, my miracle babies, thank you for the gift of motherhood, for teaching me to live in the moment, for blowing my ideas of good parenting right out of the water, and for making sure our lives are always loud and joyous. Thank you for humbling me with your unwavering love.

Mom and Dad, thank you for guiding the way with your good example, by showing me with your unrelenting love and support that I can do anything that I aspire to achieve.

Thank you to my sister, Megan, for taking the leap into motherhood alongside me. Sisterhood was given to us, but our friendship is something we have chosen, despite the pancakes! Thanks for teaching me all you know about boobs to help make this book great.

And to Meghan, thank you for taking this leap of faith with me. By turning our midday school office banter into a reality, the career dreams I never knew I had have come true. Thank you for your brutal honesty, your friendship, a listening ear, and toiling alongside me with no intention of ever giving up on the community that we have created together.

**meghan says**

Thank you to my partner in crime, Matt, for making marriage and this twin parenting gig pretty sweet. Thanks for going "all in" on a life with me, for tag teaming thousands of diaper changes at 3 a.m., for early morning dance parties, and for reminding me to brush my teeth when I was in the trenches as a new twin mom. Most important, thank you for being my lobster.

Thank you to John and Max, my world, my miracle IVF twin boys, for keeping me on my toes, making me second-guess my mom decisions, making me come up with wacky songs in the middle of the night, and mostly for making me enjoy this wild ride called motherhood. Thank you for teaching me what true unconditional love looks like. I *love* being your mother; it's the most rewarding role I have ever stepped into.

Thank you to my mom and dad for setting the bar pretty darn high in the parenting department, showing me that hard work does pay off, making me understand the importance of carrying out commitments, and making our family extremely fun to grow up in. You're crushing it as grandparents! Let's just hope your "little lump of sugar" can live up to your name!

Thank you to my sister, Holly, my very best friend and role model, for keeping me grounded and sending me a wine delivery when I've had a hell of a week filled with mom fails. Thanks to you and your wife, Connie, for keeping it real and keeping life in perspective for me.

And finally, thank you, Jenn. We went from banking ideas off each other to turning our ideas into a reality, one we never could have dreamt would become what it has. Thank you for taking a risk with this idea. You're one in a million.

**M+J**

To the *Two Came True* readers and followers, you are gold! Thanks for hanging in there with us through the ups and downs of parenting, because Lord knows we don't have it all together, but we are in this thing as a team!

To the contributors who shared your stories with us, we are so grateful. Your input and insight have added immeasurable value for all twin parents-to-be. Thank you!

Thank you, Callisto family, for believing us to be the voices that support the families who are expecting twins and simply looking for a place to connect.

# About the Authors

**Jennifer Bonicelli** and **Meghan Hertzfeldt** are the founders of *Two Came True*, the popular website where they blog candidly about parenting, raising multiples, sleep challenges, and all things in between. Parents of multiples often experience unique situations with their kids and need different strategies than parents with a singleton. Slowly but surely, they have found ways to navigate their crazy lives with twins. Meghan and Jenn find it empowering and inspiring to help other parents of multiples know that they have someone to relate to. They offer an authentic outlet for other twin parents who are looking to connect and find support through the blog's informative, relatable, and inspiring content. With their candid yet positive voices, Meghan and Jenn have given countless overwhelmed parents the confidence they need to successfully embark on parenting twins. Jenn and Meghan have been published online at *Today, Pregnant Chicken, TwinGo Carrier, Multiples Illuminated*, and *Multiples & More*.

+ Website: TwoCameTrue.com
+ Facebook: facebook.com/twocametrueblog
+ Instagram: instagram.com/twocametrue
+ Pinterest: pinterest.com/twocametrue
+ Twitter: twitter.com/twocametrue

Jenn, a Colorado native, ventured to Santa Clara University in California to earn a bachelor of science in political science and a bachelor of arts in Spanish. She later returned home to complete her master's degree in curriculum and instruction at the University of Denver. She currently lives in Denver, Colorado, with her husband, Jordan; twin boys, Dominic and Matteo; and their wildly energetic springer, Bella. As a family of four, they are living their best life!

Meghan earned her bachelor's degree in communications from the University of Colorado at Boulder, and later completed her master's degree in elementary education at Simmons College in Boston. She currently lives in Fort Collins, Colorado, with her husband, Matt; twin sons, John and Max; and black lab, Cash. Their adventures are only getting better as a family of four.